This is a letter to the author from a long-term client, an 80-year-old married woman who "lost" her husband 20 years ago—as the primary decision maker—when he had a severe accident that left him totally disabled. This is a demonstration of the durability and practicality of the Widow's Bridge® process presented in this book, THE COMING WIDOW BOOM: What You and Your Loved Ones Can Do to Prepare for the Unthinkable.

Dear Buddy,

In response to your question about what advice I would give to someone faced with the loss of a spouse, I would say:

Doing nothing—being distracted by daily life and not keeping informed—is the worst thing one can do.

While it is true that I didn't lose my husband Don as a result of his accident, I did lose the security of the primary decision maker. I knew very little about finances, taxes, insurance, or investments. Don had always been the decision maker in our family, and that was fine with me.

The event that triggered panic in me was trying to get information from the military about Don's insurance, allotments, and pay. They refused to give me any information. Our daughter, a Lieutenant Colonel, stepped in to get paper work started so I could gain access to his personal records.

Actually, my biggest concern was changing roles. I was totally unprepared. I had to make all the plans and decisions about everything. Perhaps this is what most widows fear—intimidation. I had become the primary caregiver in an instant, without the skills required to be effective. Strategies in your program, the Widow's Bridge®, helped me in my process to change roles.

What I found most unsettling was inaction. Vacillation back and forth between being anxious about ongoing medical problems and not knowing enough about finances made life very difficult. It was fortunate that you and I had already established a "trusted advisor" relationship. As I recall, the first thing to be done was to establish protection for Don in case something would happen to me.

Looking back, the most interesting part of what we've accomplished is that all decisions followed a plan. Many time~ ~~u have recommended that I review where my money goes and what my l   ~ -till take this action, though I don't dwell on money.

When we established the generatior   ;h my 80th year. I shared this with a frien₵   to do after 80. Darned if I'm not close to   ₵ to do after 100.

The Widow's Bridge® has pointed out the importance of staying involved with family assets and liabilities. I'm still healthy and in great shape for 80. Don is involved as much as possible at 85, but any decision is still mine. Planning ahead is a must.

Buddy, it seems as if I've done the Widow's Bridge® strategies all along. You must have trained me well, because I had already shifted priorities for our assets. We discussed paying off the mortgage on our home. That action is under way and will not affect any current investments. Plans are to simplify daily living and make decisions about how personal and household possessions are distributed. This will relieve some of the burden to the family when Don and I are gone.

The next action, using the "Superplan® Progress Reporter," is to look closely at how to protect current investments and to allocate funds to reduce my taxable income. Is a trust for our grandchildren the best? Can I do it with pretax money? Also, what difficulties are ahead if I loan family members money? Many times this leaves repercussions if not done properly.

Back to square one? Not quite! However, it is back to the future focus. It seems to me that we've taken this step before. Using the "Superplan® Future Focus" worksheet, I have filled out each segment. The value in doing this is:

1. *It provides the backbone to my plans.*
2. *It helps focus decisions.*
3. *It shows me where I need to get appropriate help.*

Buddy, I guess this is the long way to say the following: The Widow's Bridge® outlines very specific actions needed and provides helpful guidelines that are easy to follow. What I have learned is this:

1. *Planning is essential and having a strategic plan to follow is a must. Everyone needs to plan ahead so not to be too overwhelmed when roles change.*

2. *The Widow's Bridge® outlines the necessity of staying informed. Changing situations can be a second trauma if unprepared to make new adjustments. Reviewing and evaluating are ongoing activities.*

3. *Using the Superplan® Model provided has made the task of looking at the future, making strategic decisions, and putting them into action in an organized fashion much easier.*

4. *Nothing is really final. However, as we move into different stages in life, it is reassuring to know that the format is reliable and always available when changes are needed. "The bridge" to making complex decisions is always there.*

As the old saying goes, "Give a man a fish, he'll eat for a day, teach a man to fish, he'll eat for a lifetime." Thank you for teaching this woman to fish.

Ruth

THE
COMING WIDOW
BOOM

What You and Your Loved Ones Can Do to Prepare for the Unthinkable

*A practical path
to financial and emotional wellness
now and after the loss of a loved one.*

By
JAMES F. (BUDDY) THOMAS, JR.

Robert D. Reed Publishers • Bandon, OR

Robert D. Reed Publishers
P.O. Box 1992
Bandon, OR 97411
Phone: 541-347-9882 • Fax: -9883
E-mail: 4bobreed@msn.com
web site: www.rdrpublishers.com

Author Photo: **Rebecca Lawson**
Cover Designer: **Cleone Lyvonne**
Cover Photo: "Enjoying life while working at the beach"
© Ximagination, Fotolia.com
Editor: **Cleone Lyvonne**
Typesetter: **Barbara Kruger**

ISBN 978-1-931741-75-0

Library of Congress Control Number 2006927472

Manufactured, typeset and printed in the United States of America

This book is dedicated to my wonderful wife, Liz (who will most likely outlive me), and our parents.

My mother, Ann Thomas, who taught me, as a child, how to respect and empathize with women in her home-based beauty salon.

My dad, Jim Thomas, who beat the odds, outlived his wife of 54 years, and courageously carried on.

My father-in-law, George Coates, who passed away before his time, leaving a family behind.

And, my mother-in-law, Mary Coates, who kept her family together on her own in spite of her plight.

ACKNOWLEDGMENTS

Robert Reed and Cleone Lyvonne for seeing the value to all couples

Paul McEwen, Esq., and Jim Perich, CPA, for their wisdom, experience, expertise, and confidence

All of the client families of Superior Planning for their trust, and their business

The widows and widowers who participated in the survey for their faith in me and our firm

The accountants, attorneys, and other professionals who participated in the survey for their insights

The staff at Superior Planning, Amy, Carol, and Jamie, for their dedication

My wife Liz, and my sons, Dominic and George, for their patience, understanding, support, and love

Dan Sullivan and the staff at The Strategic Coach and my fellow participants

Curtis Verstraete at The Bishop Information Group, Inc.

Robert Stuberg, Theresa Papparella, Joan Huyser-Honig, and Pamela J. Forsberg at The Strategic Publisher

TABLE OF CONTENTS

All progress begins by telling the truth.

— Dan Sullivan

Ready or not, here it comes... The Widow Boom! From the time the first of their generation was born to the present day, the World War II baby boomers have created radical social and economic paradigm shifts shaping the culture of our world. Their deaths will be no different.

This book is about what may be the most radical boomer shift of all. Currently focusing on retirement, one of the most significant life events thereafter for them will be the death of a spouse. A well-documented projection is that more than $41 trillion ($41,000,000,000,000) will be inherited by their children.

However, another remarkable yet less-known statistic points to the fact that before their children receive it, the balance of financial power will shift in an unexpected way. Women traditionally survive their husbands 80% of the time; and on average, they outlive them for about fourteen years. The obvious conclusion is that these "Widow Boomers" will control the lion's share of the greatest wealth the world has ever known for decades before passing it on to the next generation.

I am sure that the social and economic implications of this situation will be talked and written about for years to come, but those issues are beyond the scope of this text.

You might ask, "Isn't it a little early to be worrying about this now?" Though it may seem premature, as you will see, preparing for this event will take some time. And the average age of a widow is surprisingly only 56, 25% of whom are under 45. It is not too soon to plan.

The first edition of this book, **The Widow's Bridge: The Surviving Spouse's Guide To Emotional and Financial Well-Being,** was written for widows and their trusted advisors. As more and more widows had read it and followed the Widow's Bridge® process, the most common response I heard from them was along the lines of, "I wish I had some idea about what to expect <u>before</u> it happened."

Also, couples that read that book have used it as a strategic planning tool and for talking points as they worked on developing their family's estate plans. They told me it was a valuable resource in helping them focus on and work through what many people have found unimaginable.

One couple even asked if we could have a meeting with the two of them and pretend the husband had already died. The rules were as follows: Our firm would act as if the husband wasn't in the room (dead), and he was not allowed to talk during the meeting. Then we would proceed to address the issues that she would be facing if he were actually gone.

These experiences inspired this second edition, **The Coming Widow Boom: What You and Your Loved Ones Can Do to Prepare for the Unthinkable**. It is in that light that I suggest you read this book, as an imaginary journey of what life might be like if the unthinkable had happened to you last week.

Warning: This is not an exercise in morbidity. It is an objective drill of what could and most likely will happen some day. Please note that this exercise is for you when you are 100% committed to your relationship.

Reading this book and facing the potential of this relatively inevitable event now, before it happens, while you are both alive, capable of making important decisions, and have time to adjust, will go a long way toward making the task more manageable when it occurs.

As you will read, many widows have described their initial position as being on the edge of a great unknown, a psychological gap in their lives with no idea of *how* or even *if* they will make it to the *other side* where they hope to confidently move on with their lives. As you take your imaginary journey across the Widow's Bridge®, imagine yourself alone, your life partner gone, unavailable to help you as you face the challenges of widowhood. Also, remember the actual journey will be even more difficult as the problems you face will be real and the grief overwhelming.

If you already are a widow, this book will be more than an imaginary journey for you. It will be your reality. Use this book as a blue print, a reference guide, or both to put both you and your trusted advisor on the same page (both figuratively and literally). It will provide you with insight into what is referred to as the Widow's Plight Gap and offers a plan to follow during the time this approximately two-year condition is most prevalent—a map that will lead you from uncertainty to confidence.

In our survey of widows and advisors, we heard two repeating themes, one from each perspective—the widow and her advisors.

Widow: My advisor (attorney, CPA, etc.) doesn't understand what I am going through… sometimes it's impossible to think clearly.

Advisor: My client can't seem to make a decision… this makes it very difficult for me to do my job.

If you are a surviving spouse, give a copy of this book to your trusted advisor.

If you are the trusted advisor, give a copy of this book to every couple: your own family members, clients, friends, and acquaintances.

Whether you are a widow already, or a man or woman having the courage to think about the *unthinkable* and communicate with your spouse now BEFORE it happens, reading and planning your future using *The Coming Widow Boom* will be an empowering experience that will give you peace, security, and confidence.

A Special Message for the Recently Widowed and Their Trusted Advisor

Back in the 1940s, a common tradition was for widows to wear black armbands for a period of time after their spouses passing so that those they encountered would be aware of their fragile condition and treat them accordingly. In today's get-over-it world, the community may not be as sensitive; but the trauma, pain, and potential state of the surviving spouse that we call The Widow's Plight Gap is no less extreme.

Those survivors who have used The Widow's Bridge® process and successfully carried on with their lives had told us the three most important things they have done to move forward were:

1. Accept their condition and take personal responsibility for their lives.
2. Identify their professional trusted advisor to guide them through their plight.
3. Do at least one task regarding their plan, however small, per day.

The professional advisors who have facilitated The Widow's Bridge® process tell us the keys to a successful transition for the survivors they have worked with were:

1. Allowing enough time to grieve, heal, learn, and make progress (about two years).
2. Trusting the advisor to hold their hand and coordinate their advisory team.
3. Maintaining contact, usually weekly, that established a pace and built momentum.

The Widow's Bridge® process is the only proven, comprehensive program available, with a beginning and an end, for surviving spouses and their trusted advisors to work together to overcome the paralysis and pain of The Widow's Plight Gap, to become more financially secure, and to move on, with confidence, to the next stage of their lives.

The Ten Myths of Widowhood

1. **MYTH:** *Because my spouse and I have an estate plan, I'm done.* The truth is that plans made while both spouses are alive are naturally incomplete. The survivor completes the plan.

2. **MYTH:** *Do nothing for a year.* State and federal laws require certain actions during the first year. Other prudent decisions are not only necessary but can be healthy.

3. **MYTH:** *The legal aspect is the most important.* This is only one of the three vital aspects of every financial plan.

4. **MYTH:** *The tax-accounting aspect is the most important.* This is also one of the three vital aspects of every financial plan.

5. **MYTH:** *The investment aspect is the most important.* Again, this is one of the three vital aspects and none of the three can be *the most important.* They are all very important.

6. **MYTH:** *My kids are my best source of support.* Court cases abound due to conflicts of interest between what is emotional support and personal financial agenda.

7. **MYTH:** *My friends are my best source of support.* Honorable and not-so-honorable intentions are no substitute for sound objective professional advice.

8. **MYTH:** *There's not that much to work with.* It is 100% of what you have.

9. **MYTH:** *There is nothing I can do about it.* If not you, who?

10. **MYTH:** *There is no one I can trust.* Finding a trustworthy advisor may be your most important task.

Rising From the Ashes

This book was written during the wildfires that devastated Southern California. My neighborhood was one of those that was surrounded by fire. The devastation of the property and woodlands around us was extensive. The day after the fires the landscape, including a forest of 60-foot eucalyptus trees, was a black and gray, smoldering, ashen, lifeless scene. I saw the remnants of this tragedy every day as I drove to and from my office. Within three months, bright green sprouts appeared from the black ground beneath what was left of the trees. On this daily drive through the forest, I was impressed by the steady rebirth of nature. Within another month, leaves began sprouting from the charred trunks of the trees and the ground became like a bright green-velvet carpet amid an otherwise bleak scene. Within 6 months, the new growth began to overtake what was once bleakness as a new character arose from the forest. The ashes had fertilized the area to a richness even greater than before. After two years, the forest was almost completely renewed; the remnants of the devastation, though still apparent, only added to its new character and beauty.

—James F. (Buddy) Thomas, Jr.

Before you read further, let me elaborate upon some potentially sensitive points. It is with thoughtful deliberation that my editors and I have made conscious editorial decisions faced by every author.

To protect their privacy, I have altered the names and some of the circumstances of my clients and their families. My professional colleagues have granted me permission to use their real names. I am grateful to the many clients and friends who have shared their experiences with me for this book. In sharing other widows' stories, my hope is that you will realize you are not alone and will seek to find creative ways through your individual situation.

I want to assure my readers that I intend no insult in using the female or masculine tense selectively. In writing this book, using gender-neutral language seemed impractical. At the risk of offending anyone, as the author I found it necessary to select a gender for clarity, and to avoid confusion and clumsy writing. Therefore, I selected the female gender for the surviving spouse and male gender for the trusted advisor. Of course, the surviving spouse and professional advisor bear no specific gender, and I mean no offense in making an editorial choice for purposes of writing this book. The Widow's Bridge® process presented in this book is for both the widow and widower.

Whatever we are waiting for—peace of mind,
contentment, grace, the inner awareness
of simple abundance—it will surely come to us,
but only when we are ready to receive it
with an open and grateful heart.

— Sarah Ban Breathnach

"What do I do now?" As a surviving spouse this is the most important question you can ask. It is a difficult one because it is very uncomfortable to talk about how to pick up the pieces after your spouse dies—sometimes even with your closest confidant.

You are now the sole person responsible to settle your husband's estate and work through complex financial, legal, and personal issues as you go through one of the most difficult periods in your life. As the leader of your family's financial matters, you must consider how these issues correspond with your family's emotional and physical well-being. You must make all these decisions without your life-partner and the loyal support he provided.

My name is Buddy Thomas, and this book is based on over 25 years of experience in working to help families reestablish themselves after a spouse died. Since 1982, as a life insurance agent, registered investment advisor, and certified financial planner, I have helped hundreds of families move from financial dependence, to financial independence, to "the ultimate stage of planning"—financial transcendence—when families focus on taking their legacy beyond financial security. Being a trusted advisor for numerous financially independent families, I learned first-hand the impact that the death of a spouse has on the family.

Early in the first year of losing your spouse, you will begin to experience the Widow's Plight Gap. This is also when you begin to cope with the emotional grief of your loss, you realize that you are alone to protect yourself and your wealth, and you must start to create a brighter future for you and your family. It is the time to look at your family in the present, and for you to redefine the future—the one you envision (even if you can't see it right now).

Heartache can "paralyze" you for a period of time. This is natural. Grieving is a normal human condition and an essential aspect of your well-being. Coping with your loss is something you must face mostly alone, in your own time.

Let me reassure you that you are not alone. Women generally outlive their husbands. Life expectancy at 60 years of age for women is 83 and for men 78. However, 56 is now the average age of a widow. (A Working Woman Guide To Financial Security; www.urbanext.uiuc.edu/ww1/00-01.html). Nearly 700,000 women lose their husbands each year and will be widows for an average of 14 years (U.S. Bureau of Census–1999). Relative to estate settlement issues, $41 trillion is estimated to change hands between husbands, wives, and their heirs during the next 55 years (www.morethanmoney.org/

articles/mtm32_schervish.pdf). The majority of these dealings will fall on the shoulders of a widow. On average there are four times as many widows (8.4 million) as widowers (1.9 million) as reported in 1999 by American Association of Retired Persons. Thirty-two percent of women aged 55 and older are widows, and only 9 percent of men aged 55 and older are widowers (2000 U.S. Census). In 2002 alone there were 800,000 new widows/widowers in the United States (National Mental Health Association).

Whether financially independent or not, there are similar challenges every surviving spouse faces. However, for the financially independent—meaning your income from your investments exceeds your lifestyle expenses— tackling your financial affairs is distinctively problematic because of the complexity of the decisions to be made.

Most families have done some level of financial and estate planning, but now going at it alone, you may lack complete confidence in taking control of your future. Your goals may not be clear and you may lack a reasonable plan for moving forward. You may not fully understand your financial, legal, and administrative responsibilities. You may not know how to best provide for your family's financial needs. In addition, there is probably fear of the unknown and too much information coming your way. And all of this happens under the cloak of grief as you experience the Widow's Plight Gap.

The good news is every surviving spouse can take control of her life and financial well-being. However, it requires professional help and a guided path to get you out of the darkness and into the light where new goals can be seen.

Very few surviving spouses who attempt to go it alone—without a trusted advisor—will make a complete transition. With the amount of personal, business, and fiduciary issues that you must muddle through, now more than ever, you need a professional with certain technical skills and abilities to hold your hand. Typically this will be a CPA, estate planning lawyer, financial planner, or life insurance agent. Often the professional was the family's trusted advisor prior to the spouse's death.

Be aware that the professional you trust may be a specialist in one field, e.g., CPA, lawyer, investment advisor, etc. Surviving spouse transition is also a specialty. If your trusted advisor does not have surviving spouse transition experience, he can either learn as he goes or use the Widow's Bridge® process presented in this book.

This book is designed to be a resource for you as well as your trusted advisor. It will walk you through how to deal with the formidable challenge of transitioning from a lifetime of established habits, some that no longer apply, to a new operating system that can position you and your family for a prosperous, vibrant future. Also provided are checklists and a timeline of what must be done, and what can be done to prepare for imminent times of decision making. You will find these lists will help you set a course and keep you on track, plus they provide a positive "distraction therapy." This transition program is one of the few constructive activities available to deal with and actually prosper from experiencing the Widow's Plight Gap.

Through the years, I also observed a stunning trend. I realized that the statistics are true: My male clients were retiring from this earth well before their wives. When the husband died, the wife realized she had to rely on someone to trust who genuinely understood and could help her manage her multifaceted, inexplicably-complicated financial situation. I became the person to hold her hand and walk with her through this time. It was no small task.

Over time I noticed patterns in the surviving spouses' experiences. I also recognized how critical it is for a surviving spouse to have a trusted professional who understands the complexity of her situation and will take the lead on guiding her through the daunting ordeal. There are a magnitude of issues to deal with if a surviving spouse wants to maintain her independence, continue receiving income, preserve the family integrity and wealth, and move forward with confidence.

As a result of my years of experience, I pioneered the only known transitional program for the surviving spouse that comprehensively addresses all the vital issues. The Widow's Bridge® helps the family decision maker overcome her loss, control her income, protect her wealth, and build a successful future. It has been used to successfully guide many surviving spouses through this major life event.

To more completely understand the widow's dilemma, I also conducted an extensive, one-on-one survey composed of interviews with those whom I had worked with, and an equal number I had not. In this survey, the surviving spouses said that financial and emotional stability are interrelated. If you have one and not the other, in most instances eventually you end up with neither. Financial instability can lead to emotional instability. Conversely, emotional instability often leads to significant financial loss.

Interviews were also conducted with other trusted advisors—CPAs, estate planning lawyers, certified financial planners, investment advisors, and life insurance agents—about the real life situations their surviving spouse clients had faced. These professionals verbalized a need for a process that genuinely aids the surviving spouse during this complicated time of getting back on her feet.

From the insight of widows and their trusted advisors, the Widow's Bridge® process was created. Let this process be your and your trusted advisor's guide in managing your transition so that you will realize financial security and contentment in the next stage of your life. Use the techniques in this book to help you get both feet firmly planted on the ground and position yourself to move forward at your own pace, toward your own vision.

CHAPTER ONE

The Widow's Plight

*I was becoming confused as I realized
my husband was gone. It was like someone suddenly
turned out the lights and people began shouting at me,
telling me what to do from all different directions
as I stood alone in the dark.*

— surviving spouse survey participant

Losing your spouse will be one of the most difficult,
life-altering times in your life. Know that you will get
through this period. Trust that what you are experiencing
is normal.

Every surviving spouse goes through similar challenges.
Within the first two years after losing your partner you
will face some form, or forms, of the temporary condition,
the Widow's Plight Gap.

During the Widow's Plight Gap, you face dark moments of sorrow before you get to the other side, which is to experience a "different" kind of happiness. Grief teaches you to let go of familiar habits and shows you how life has changed. You realize you must now deal with all your responsibilities and your spouse's previous responsibilities. You have fiduciary responsibilities in settling your spouse's estate. Financial responsibilities must be tackled. You must manage solicited, and unsolicited, advice. It is a period of unanticipated, time-consuming, complicated surprises. It is when you begin to look at your family in the present, and then choose to let the future merely happen, or you begin to deliberately create a future based on who you are and what you envision.

Family and friends provide support by listening. However, no one can fully understand what you are going through. And the truth is, most don't know how to interact with you, and many can't take the time out of their busy lives to empathize with you. To compound the situation, there are no shortcuts to stop the pain. Over time, however, it does slowly fade. But in the meantime, there is simply no easy way around this piercingly painful period of your life.

Few people understand the legitimate concerns you have for your well-being, both emotional and financial. This is especially true for the financially independent widow who carries the stigma that money is not a "concern." To the contrary, your financial resources bring numerous issues to contend with that will affect the fabric of your deepest emotional well-being.

As you attempt to cross the Widow's Plight Gap, you will likely face three primary potential losses: 1) your independence, 2) your income, and 3) your ability to help your family. Each dilemma is a very real concern. If ignored, one or any combination can negatively impact your life.

Dilemma #1: Losing Your Independence

The "dawn of the new day" brings a slow awakening to the fact that you can lose your independence and freedom to live your life your way. It may be psychologically impossible to maintain your existing home and lifestyle. Family members may feel they need to take care of you whether the need is there or not. Those around you may begin to try to dictate how and even where you live.

It is common to feel apprehension about making decisions as you move through this daunting life change. However, if you let someone control your assets and your dreams, they have the potential to control your choices. Lack of self-reliance leads to loss of self-esteem and dignity. Unless you clearly communicate and stand firm about your desires, your family or other influential people may believe they need to intervene. Even those with the best intentions probably won't know how to give you what you need and want most. There is also the potential underlying risk that an assisting "supporter" won't have your best intentions in mind.

As you move through your grief, be aware that your personal growth can be stifled until you decide to take control of your life. This will not be the last time you will need to draw upon your courage as you move forward.

Take time to mourn your loss and reflect on the past while living only in the emotion—for the moment. You do not need to progress hastily to have a vibrant life again. Rather, be conscious of your need for independence and know that eventually it will be necessary to define what you want—on your terms.

Allow yourself time to grieve. Just realize that it becomes unhealthy when your personal growth is stopped for a significant length of time. Grieving is a natural process that enables you to learn how to deal with your deepest emotions. However, during periods of sorrow, it is also important to not let it rob you of living. Instead gain strength from the experience whenever possible.

Sharon's Story

Sharon's husband didn't come home after going to the hospital with indigestion, which turned out to be a symptom of serious internal complications. Until that event, she and her husband enjoyed a life working together in their boutique shop as a hobby. Semi-retired in San Diego after their son took over their development business, life was good. They had a comfortable routine. They had been partners in life and business. However, the finances had been her husband's responsibility. Sharon knew little about the finances and was not comfortable making these decisions.

During the first year after her husband's death, she had no idea what to do with her finances, or her life. Her son was the one person she trusted. However, she began to realize that his involvement was not in her best interest. Although he had good intentions, Sharon felt that his ideas of what would make her happy would overpower hers. She feared she would become dependent on him for everything, even to the point of having to ask him for her money.

It was not until Sharon felt that her life was getting out of control and not going in her chosen direction that she got the courage to take charge and make her own decisions. She realized she had to trust someone other than her son. She had to trust someone who could give her professional financial guidance. This is when she found herself talking to me. I began to walk her across the Widow's Bridge®. This step-by-step program helped her sort out the important details and gain clarity. Within six months she turned her life around by making the necessary decisions to live independently. It wasn't an easy transition, but she is now living with financial and personal freedom, making sound choices for herself, living with the consequences, and building confidence daily.

Dilemma #2: Losing Your Income

The loss of your spouse's income, estate transfer costs, and the mishandling of assets, income, and expenses can negatively impact your investment portfolio—the engine that generates your lifestyle income. Comforts you enjoyed with your spouse may be at risk. It will take time to become fully aware of the impact your spouse's death had on your income. Unfortunately, much of this awareness will come in the form of surprises.

At times you may feel overwhelmed with how to identify and solve complex issues as you take control of your finances. Unless you were previously involved in the details of these matters, you probably have little knowledge of the process your spouse used to make decisions about asset management, and income and expense cash flow. Furthermore, without extensive personal financial planning experience, you are likely unaware of all the options available to you. It is also unlikely that you know which options apply to your situation. A worse case scenario is when finances are completely unorganized and virtually impossible to piece together.

When you do not have a road map to guide you to your financial future, you have to create one—sometimes without knowing where you want to go. If a plan is already in place, it is based on assumptions before your spouse's death. Your task now is to execute it under today's conditions. This means that it may need to be modified based on your new solo lifestyle and new assumptions about the future that call for renewed forethought.

Oma was introduced to me by a colleague after her husband died. Her income and lifestyle were up against a ticking clock that had been ignored. Her husband had been a successful entrepreneur who sold his business for an installment note. The note was bringing in many thousands of dollars a month and was their primary source of income. When we met we determined the note had only two years remaining, and then the money would stop coming in. Furthermore, there was no other source of income. To make matters more complicated, she was subsidizing the lifestyles of her adult children; a significant portion of the monthly income was used to maintain their excessively comfortable existence. The family's current lifestyle could only be sustained for the term of the note, and Oma had no plan for her financial well-being thereafter. If she took no action, she would have no income in two years.

Oma decided to take control of her life. Following the Widow's Bridge® process, she began to lay the groundwork for a brighter future. She determined the lifestyle she could afford and began to spend within her means. She took advantage of our experience and guidance to rearrange her remaining assets and create a solid blueprint for managing them. She soon had the income to support herself indefinitely. Her actions also forced her children to live within their means, which in turn has helped them on their paths to independence.

Dilemma #3: Losing the Ability to Help Your Family

As if life didn't hand you enough with having to manage the grief of losing your spouse and dealing with enormous financial concerns, you also realize that the security of your children, grandchildren, and others you care about may be at risk. Having the sole responsibility of parenthood, grandparenthood, and primary benefactor can be formidable. And surviving spouses without family heirs are not unscathed. They too face dissolution of their legacy.

Since each heir has different needs and wants, there is a real possibility some will not obtain the desired benefits in terms of money and control they expect from the estate. There may be confusion over responsibilities and fairness, which can bring disruptive misunderstandings. These misunderstandings can cause hurt that festers and a breakdown in relationships that can take years to repair, if ever.

Polarization of those involved may be on the verge of taking place or may have already happened. Infighting suddenly becomes the family social activity that can sadly alter a family structure at its very core. Disputes can lead to the dissolution of the family's financial security, and most destructive of all, to its value base. All of this can harmfully interrupt the grieving process. In time, the momentum of your family's growth can be slowed, or stopped all together. Furthermore, the funds targeted for education, social causes, and other lofty purposes may be co-opted for other needs.

Richard, an litigation lawyer in Southern California who was interviewed for this book, shares the following story of one of his clients:

Rachel inherited the family business worth more than $10 million from her husband when he died. Two of her three adult children were involved in the business. Initially, thinking she was not capable of managing the affairs of the estate settlement, she turned the matter over to her children to work out the details themselves. The ensuing disagreements and infighting forced the sale of the company with more than 90 percent of the proceeds going to settlement and legal costs. As of this writing, none of the children are speaking to each other, and the estate has yet to be settled.

One thing Sharon, Oma, and Rachel each realized is that they could not do it on their own. Sharon and Oma took the leap of faith and trusted a professional to walk with them through the darkness and confusion one step at a time. Rachel, unfortunately, did not make this choice. As demonstrated in their stories above, their choices made a significant difference in their futures.

Begin your process by believing in yourself. Have faith and hope that the future will be brighter. Take some time to discern who will be your trusted advisor—someone who has the acumen to follow a surviving spouse transition strategy that will take you through this complex phase in your life. Then, exercise the courage to take action and make progress towards your new future.

CHAPTER TWO

Who Can You Trust?

You may be deceived if you trust too much,
but you will live in torment if you don't trust enough.

— Frank Crane

If you are worried about losing your independence, your income, or your ability to help loved ones, you might be tempted to sit tight and do nothing for a while. You wouldn't be the first widow or widower to make that choice. Facing complex emotional and financial issues alone is almost impossible.

Yet not facing these issues increases the chances that your fears will come true. Every surviving spouse must wrestle with how to support her lifestyle without eroding assets needed to generate income. Because your situation is unique, you may have other challenges. Maybe you are now responsible for the family business. Perhaps your spouse made other commitments you must honor. And what about unforeseen issues?

I recently spoke with seven lawyers about times they have seen surviving spouses get into deep trouble. One guy said, "Buddy, any time I've seen a probate process that really went wrong, it's been because the surviving spouse seemed paralyzed. She never asked anyone, 'What do I do now? Will you help me?'"

The other lawyers around the table agreed. "The ones who never ask for help simply don't know who to trust," another explained.

This chapter will help you evaluate which professional is best suited to become your trusted advisor.

Trusting Is Your Key to Moving Forward

There are two parts to trust relationships. You, as the surviving spouse, must have the ability to trust. And the person you turn to during this crisis must be trustworthy.

As my lawyer friends noticed in their clients' experience, having the ability to trust is hugely important. But for some people it is not that easy. First, ask yourself whether you are able to trust. If not, what stands in your way?

If you are like the widows I have worked with, you probably feel very vulnerable right now. You might even wonder whether the advisor you seek out will be more interested in your wealth than in you. Yet, as so many widows have unhappily discovered, it is even more risky to trust no one.

Experts worth trusting to assist you with your financial and legal responsibilities must deserve your confidence. You will be seeking their advice for at least the next two years as you overcome your loss, take control of your income, protect your wealth, and position yourself for a successful future.

Even in your present state of grief, you still have the ability to choose well. The following pages describe four key characteristics that identify whom you can trust. Our simple quiz will help you compare potential trusted advisors.

Look for These Four Qualities

You might begin by calling a financial planner, lawyer, investment advisor, accountant, or another specialist already familiar with your family values and finances. Or perhaps you will ask another widow to recommend professionals who helped her through difficult times. In any event, you will want to look for people who you believe truly care about you and who display qualities of genuine expertise, dependability, responsiveness to your needs, and a priority of your interest over theirs.

*(In **The Trusted Advisor**, an excellent book for high-level professionals, authors David H. Maister, Charles H. Green, and Robert M. Galford, express trust as a formula: the sum of credibility, reliability and intimacy—divided by self-orientation.)*

Genuine Expertise

It is likely that most potential advisors you choose to meet with will have the credentials—education, years of experience, and so on—to address many of your questions. But what do they do with this knowledge? Experts who ask technically pertinent questions show that they know what they are talking about. But you also want someone who asks you questions without being condescending, someone who genuinely cares whether you understand the issues and your options.

Experts who genuinely care about your situation will often start sharing useful information even before you have signed a contract. *The Trusted Advisor* describes someone who needed to hire a firm to probate a will. Some firms focused on their expertise and fees. Finally one lawyer asked, "How much do you know about probating a will?" When the inquirer answered, "Nothing," the lawyer offered to fax a process outlining the steps. He also included relevant phone numbers. This was all provided for free— before the lawyer received any business.

Experts worth your trust will illustrate how they might help you plan for the future, rather than simply assert, "We'll take care of it for you." They are honest, freely admitting when they don't know an answer.

Referrals from people you trust are strong indicators that you have found a genuine expert. Paul McEwen, a top-notch estate-planning lawyer, is humble. He is excellent at explaining things from a client's point of view. That is extremely powerful in building trust. Paul's clients trust him when he says, "I'll help you with legal issues. You need someone like Buddy to help you with planning. I'll walk you over and introduce you to him." Over half of our firm's clients have come to us because of referrals like these. Look for them for yourself.

Dependability

Dependable people act consistently. They return phone calls, are on time and prepared for appointments, and they follow up with whatever information they promise. The more we experience individuals' consistent behavior, the more we view them as dependable. That is why your first strategy for finding a dependable advisor may be to contact someone you've known awhile.

This might be someone you and your spouse consulted together. Perhaps it is a professional your spouse dealt with. It might even be someone you have known in another context. For example, after an old friend of mine died, his wife phoned me. We lived over 2,000 miles apart, so her husband and I had not done any business together. She called me: "I don't know what to do." I said, "I can help you if you'll let me." She said, "Well, I guess I'll have to trust somebody. I've known you for a long time, and you've always done what you said you would."

Whether or not you have a history with a potential advisor, it is always okay to ask, "What can I expect if I work with you? How do you deliver your service? What is your process?" Ideally the advisor will also introduce the topic of fees, so you know what his services will cost.

Notice whether the advisor consistently asks about what you already know about a problem and then uses terms you understand. Does he also consult with you about what each meeting or step is designed to accomplish? Does he follow up?

Responsiveness

Since you will be working through complex, private matters with your trusted advisor, it is vital that you feel comfortable together. You need to feel that you connect or click, that you have similar values. The more you relate to someone's values and the better you feel about him, the more you'll trust him.

Look for someone who understands that your current challenges involve finances *and* emotions. You need to feel emotionally safe with your advisor. This expert should give you hope that life will get better, yet realize that in your current pain, you may only be able to deal with hard facts in small doses.

You want a compassionate person to guide you through tough dilemmas. It is your advisor's job to raise difficult issues, even if it means uncovering unpleasant surprises about the way your spouse handled the finances. Feeling a common bond with your advisor will help you weather these decisions.

A "You First" Attitude

A non-selfish outlook is the most important quality to look for in a trusted advisor. Steer clear of people who finish your sentences for you or keep bringing the conversation back to their own stories, successes, or qualifications. Of course, some stories may help you understand new, important concepts, but if you walk away from a meeting feeling like "it was all about the advisor," then beware.

The way a potential advisor asks questions gives clues about his point of view. Someone who asks closed-end questions—which allow for only a yes or no answer—may try to funnel you into a quick solution "that works for all our widows."

A new widow I'll call Bobbi turned first to an estate planning lawyer her husband had trusted. He said, "I'll send you the forms. Just fill them out."

A question on the form was "How much money was in his pockets when he died"? That hurt Bobbi so much. This was her trusted advisor, yet he had no ability to view her situation through her eyes. He just wanted to complete a process without empathizing.

Someone who really cares about helping you take responsibility for your future will ask open-ended questions. This advisor will spend enough time listening to you define the problem, checking and summarizing every so often to make sure you both understand each other.

Trustworthy advisors will put your best interests ahead of theirs. For example, someone with your level of wealth generally faces complicated financial and emotional choices. An advisor who wants the best future for you will want to talk with your other advisors. He'll care more about getting you the best answers rather than being the source of every answer.

As an aid in determining your trusted advisor, you may want to try the following exercise. Rank each question from 5 to 1 (5 being the best possible and 1 being the least). The higher the TOTAL SCORE*, the more likely the advisor deserves your trust.

EXPERTISE, DEPENDABILITY, RESPONSIVENESS

Part One | 1-5

_____ 1. This advisor has the knowledge necessary to deal with my financial, legal, and emotional situation.

_____ 2. This advisor has experienced the transition of working with a surviving spouse.

_____ 3. I have enough experience with this advisor to know he or she will follow through on promises.

_____ 4. I understand what it will be like to work with this person and believe the experience will be good.

_____ 5. This advisor shares my financial values and philosophy.

_____ **Part One Subtotal = A (maximum 25)**

A "YOU FIRST" ATTITUDE

Part Two | 6-10

_____   6. I feel emotionally safe with this person.

_____   7. This advisor is a good listener.

_____   8. He or she asks me probing questions that help me see my problems in a new light.

_____   9. This advisor will help me find the best solutions, even if it means calling in other specialists to deal with my financial, legal, or emotional complications.

_____   10. This advisor seems to care about helping me develop a solution right for me.

_____   **Part Two Subtotal = B**
(maximum 25)

_____   **Multiply B by 3 = C**
(maximum 75)

_____   **Add A and C for TOTAL SCORE***
(maximum 100)

CHAPTER THREE

Surviving
One Step at a Time

Beset by a difficult problem? Now is your chance to shine. Pick yourself up, get to work, and get triumphantly through it.

— *Ralph Marston*

Once you have chosen a trusted advisor, you have a companion to help you through the next two years. But wouldn't a map be nice? Rather than let you and your trusted advisor wade blindly into the thicket of your problems, this book offers a definitive path based on your past, present, and future.

Your path will lead through three distinct phases, but we do not expect that every surviving spouse's path will look the same. The Widow's Bridge® process will give you and your advisor some basic guidelines for taking it one step at a time—at a pace and in a direction best for you.

Three Phases

From a "big picture" view, the Widow's Bridge® process is divided into three distinct phases that are like platforms, each one supporting the next.

Phase #1: Stabilize—Assess and stabilize your current personal and financial situation.

Phase #2: Plan—Develop your new family vision, goals, and strategies.

Phase #3: Operate—Take action to implement your plan and measure its results.

THE WIDOW'S BRIDGE® SUCCESS MODEL

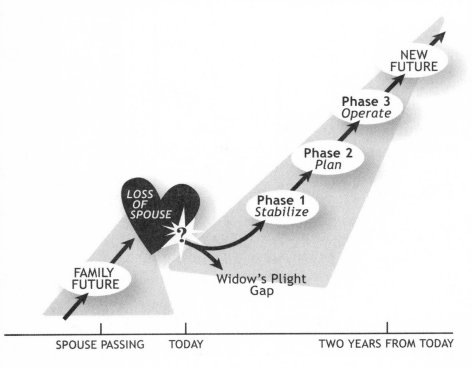

Within these phases you will climb eight steps. In the *stabilization* phase—which includes the first three steps—you will clarify your situation generally as a surviving spouse, enhance your confidence by defining the details that apply to you, and prioritize an action list of fiduciary responsibilities.

In the *plan* phase—the next three steps—you will become empowered as you inventory your resources, focus on the future, and strategize your path.

The *operate* phase—the final two steps—includes your action plan, progress report, and plan adaptions.

The following eight chapters take an in-depth look at each step, one at a time.

During the years we have helped surviving spouses, they have noticed something handy while working through each step of the three phases. The *stabilize-plan-operate* sequence works on the micro level, too. You can use this model as a planning process for any one issue, for example, managing immediate cash flow.

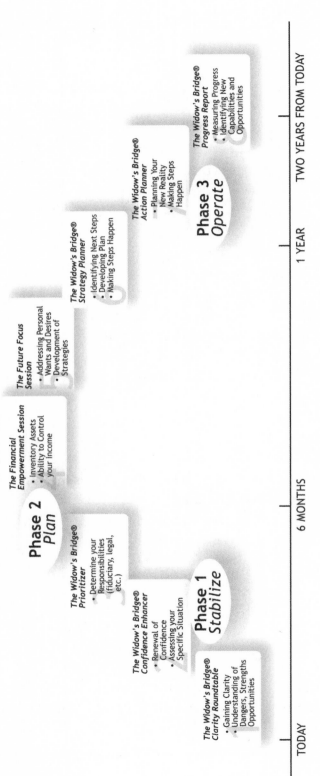

THE WIDOW'S BRIDGE® PROGRAM

Phase 1
Stabilize

*The Widow's Bridge®
Clarity Roundtable*
• Gaining Clarity
• Understanding of
  Dangers, Strengths
  Opportunities

*The Widow's Bridge®
Confidence Enhancer*
• Renewal of
  Confidence
• Assessing your
  Specific Situation

*The Widow's Bridge®
Prioritizer*
• Determine your
  Responsibilities
  (fiduciary, legal,
  etc.)

Phase 2
Plan

*The Financial
Empowerment Session*
• Inventory Assets
• Ability to Control
  your Income

*The Future Focus
Session*
• Addressing Personal
  Wants and Desires
• Development of
  Strategies

*The Widow's Bridge®
Strategy Planner*
• Identifying Next Steps
• Developing Plan
• Making Steps Happen

*The Widow's Bridge®
Action Planner*
• Planning Your
  New Reality
• Making Steps
  Happen

Phase 3
Operate

*The Widow's Bridge®
Progress Report*
• Measuring Progress
• Identifying New
  Capabilities and
  Opportunities

TODAY   6 MONTHS   1 YEAR   TWO YEARS FROM TODAY

Arlene's story will give you insight into how each macro phase flows into the next. *Arlene called me after her husband died of cancer. He was strong like John Wayne, just a tough guy. He ran the finances. She was the supporting spouse. She was expecting significant life insurance cash proceeds and was completely freaking out about what to do with it. She had no idea. So she said, "I guess I'll just use it 'til it runs out." That was her plan—until we met.*

Stabilize

First we had to stabilize her day-to-day finances so she did not use up all her precious financial resources that would eventually generate her retirement lifestyle income. Arlene had four children, all still at home. Her house was paid for. She had a small income from teaching in a parochial school. Her husband had also left her some other money, but she did not know how to use it.

There was absolutely no way she could do everything all at once. It would be too overwhelming. But if she did nothing, then a year later she'd be saying, "Nothing has changed. I feel like the money won't last. It's not getting any better." We were proactive and put first things first.

I said, "It's probably going to take us six to twelve months to get you back on your feet enough to make a plan. How much do you need a month for living expenses?" It did not take her long to get back to me. We added a thousand dollars a month to the amount she suggested, and we put a year's worth in a bank account. I said, "Each month write a check from this account—to yourself. Think of it as your paycheck."

Plan

Next we looked at the big challenges coming up. Arlene's oldest son was graduating from high school and wanted to go to a military academy. The kids were all two years apart, and she wanted to take care of her family so each could go to college. She wanted to retire by a certain age but was willing to delay that to get the kids through school.

Arlene told me what she wanted to accomplish. So we strategized a plan. As the insurance money came in, we knew the first batch could be used to supplement the first year's income. And then the second batch would be invested to generate income for ongoing revenue. Whatever was left over would go in a fund for the kid's education. We would take out education expenses as needed.

Operate

Arlene executed flawlessly. All her children graduated from college. She sold the homestead when the kids were out of the roost. She built a nice little house for her retirement. Arlene has yet to remarry, though she has an active social life. And she did not earn a lot of money as a schoolteacher. But she is set. She is a woman of independent means.

This is an over simplification of how things actually went, but the happy ending happened because Arlene developed and acted on a plan. Without a plan, she would not have had enough to last her all the way through educating her kids and still have enough principal left to generate her retirement income. She had part of her husband's retirement income but none of her own, so all the rest of her income had to come from managing this capital that she used to support her lifestyle and her kids' education. To take down principal would have taken away from the goose that was, and still is, laying golden eggs for her.

Holding Up Your End of the Deal

A recent study of people who hire financial planners showed that most clients liked their financial planner's process. But when asked to describe that process, 80 percent of them couldn't. It was enough for them to know that the planner knew how the process worked. As you might expect, though, every client was very interested in the results.

Assuming you have chosen a trusted advisor, it is important that he understands the ins and outs of the Widow's Bridge® process. You may choose, or not, whether to try and thoroughly understand each step.

A Cautionary Tale

For this process to work, however, you do need to comply with each step—so your plan has a good chance of working. We advisors occasionally hear horror stories about surviving spouses who don't move forward.

One widow was worried about losing her independence. Her husband's yacht had been his baby. She had hung out on it but did not know much about how it worked. After his death, she focused on the yacht as a way to keep her husband's spirit alive, so she got a Coast Guard pilot license. Now she knows how to run the boat, but she absolutely hates it. She realized it was his passion, not hers.

Yet she refuses to accept the fact that this yacht is not the family jewel, but the family drain. All the assets her family has—which would have been enough to support her for the rest of her life—are being eroded to maintain it. If she sells the boat and establishes some independence from her husband's choice, then the boat proceeds and other assets will be sufficient. Every day that goes by, however, those numbers grow smaller.

This woman is now completely at odds with her son. Somehow she believes that if she gives up the yacht, then her son will take over her life. She is paralyzed. While her advisor, the family CPA, was very forthright and explained the dilemma objectively, she made a promise to "think" about it, but has yet to act. A better choice might be to focus more on her philosophy, and her family and its future. A family's strength, beliefs, values, and vision can provide a foundation for an immobilized spouse to work through grief and stabilize the family.

Regain Momentum

When you lose a spouse, it is not unusual to think, "He's gone. It's done. It's over. I can't possibly remember all the things we said we would do. How will I ever carry on by myself?"

When clients first come to our firm as a couple, we encourage them to write a family financial philosophy statement. We interview the husband and wife separately. Then we sit down and show them where they differ and use those discussion points to get a better understanding of each other. We document and save their joint statement.

After a spouse dies, we can use that document to say, "This is what the two of you decided your family is about. You're not just about money. You have unique values and goals and want to provide certain support for your children and grandchildren. You've talked about a legacy to society. Simply because you have this philosophical platform, you have a lot going for you."

Perhaps you and your spouse never wrote out a family financial philosophy or vision. That is okay. Assuming you chose your trusted advisor in part because he seems to have similar values, he can also help you identify your family philosophy and clarify your vision. Now you do not have to do it all alone.

Together, over time as you *stabilize-plan-operate*, you can put some of the pieces in place. As time passes, the whole picture, like a puzzle, will naturally become clearer.

CHAPTER FOUR

Stabilize Step 1—
Gain Clarity

To solve any problem, here are three questions to ask yourself: First, what could I do? Second, what could I read? And third, who could I ask?

— Jim Rohn

When you first meet with your trusted advisor to discuss your current situation, you will probably walk in feeling very uncertain. At this initial meeting, widows have told us they feel like they are perched on the edge of the vast unknown. However, even though you may feel more fearful or uncertain than you ever have before, your advisor is there to help, and he may have even helped other widows face the same issues. Chances are you will leave this meeting believing that what you fear is in fact manageable.

In our office, we call this initial meeting the Clarity Roundtable. It is the first step in the stabilization phase. As our firm does, your trusted advisor will help you clarify your current situation by helping you take a "big picture" look at your situation and a general path to follow. The place to start is to list the dangers, opportunities, and strengths common to all widows. You can do this by discussing the five main tasks that every surviving spouse must accept and begin to see how they apply to you. You'll discover that you have inner resources and other external help to complete these tasks that you may not be aware of.

Five Major Tasks

In order to cross the Widow's Bridge®, every widow must accept responsibility to grieve, become self-sufficient in managing her lifestyle cash flow, take control of her investment portfolio, settle her husband's estate, and develop phase two of her family's legacy plan. You do not have to give equal attention to everything at once. Rather, focus on one task and then another, and you will find yourself in balance and moving forward. In fact, dealing with these general issues that every widow faces will give you the confidence to tackle your own specific challenges.

Grieve

Your first task is to accept that you must grieve. This is a very normal, necessary process that will probably go on indefinitely. We all grieve differently with essential factors rising from our personal makeup as well as our cultural and religious upbringing.

I once heard a grief counselor give a very helpful explanation of how to picture grief. She said that grief is like a huge boulder—so large and heavy that you cannot even move it. Instead, one way to deal with it is to chip away at the boulder, one little piece at a time. You keep chipping and chipping till the boulder is a rock small enough to fit in your pocket. And then you can carry it with you for the rest of your life.

Check our web site, www.widowsbridge.com, for specific recommendations on books that were written to help you chip away at your grief. These books also include helpful suggestions on purpose, nutrition, sleep, exercise, and finance.

Become Self-Sufficient

The second and third tasks of becoming self-sufficient in managing both your lifestyle cash flow and investment portfolio may seem obvious, but they represent issues that—no matter how good you are at handling them—you can always improve. You are now the sole head of the family. You and your husband used to be a team, but now you are the single individual responsible to lead the family. Without the confidant you leaned on for years, you must now take charge of all the things you used to face together.

It's now up to you to manage your lifestyle cash flow. You must also oversee your investment portfolio. Self-sufficiency comes from being in control of these fundamental aspects of life management.

Establishing yourself as an independent head of the household is the bedrock of all future decision making. Like Arlene, you know it does not all happen at once, but temporary strategies allow time for permanent plans.

The Butterfly Story

One day a young boy and his father were walking on the sidewalk when the boy noticed a caterpillar. His dad explained that it would grow into a beautiful butterfly one day. They took the caterpillar home and made a nice environment to observe its change process. The boy nurtured it and watched day after day as the cocoon formed. After an agonizingly long time, the cocoon began to crack and tiny legs appeared. The boy, feeling it was taking too long and wanting to help speed the process, cracked the cocoon so the butterfly could get out. To his shock and dismay, it died. When he told his father, his father explained that the butterfly was still too weak to live. Because it is in the struggle to get out of its cocoon that a butterfly gains strength to fly.

Settle Your Spouse's Estate

Your self-sufficiency is at the same time challenged and bolstered by the fourth task—settling the estate. There are big dangers common to widows who do not settle the estate in a timely manner. Not doing so risks losing many of the benefits of your spouse's estate plan, thus jeopardizing your income, your independence, and your status with those you love. Going through the process methodically gets the job done and also acts as an exercise to build your decision-making muscle as well as your confidence.

We use an estate settlement timeline for every surviving spouse to run on initially. For example, every widow in the United States faces three important dates after her husband's death:

The Date Probate Will Close — Probate, which means "proof of will," is the legal exercise before a court. It assures that the deceased's estate complies with state law. It is usually complicated, public, and often contentious. A normal probate takes about eighteen months. Larger estates can take much longer.

The Date the Estate Tax Return Must Be Filed — The deceased's estate must file IRS Form 706, the deceased's estate tax return, within nine months of the date of death. This applies to every estate that exceeds a certain value. If you fail to file this return and pay this federal estate tax, the IRS can place a lien on the estate for the amount owed—plus penalties and interest.

The Date the By-Pass Trusts Must Be Funded — If you have a living trust, as the surviving spouse and successor trustee, you must also transfer the deceased spouse's ownership of trust property in accordance with its terms, usually within a year of the death. The terms generally dictate that when the first spouse dies, the living trust will be split into several other trusts. You must decide how to comply with the trust and transfer the titles of the assets. There may be other restrictions as well, because these types of trusts are usually customized to pass property on to family members or to others that you and your spouse designated.

This may sound scary, but you will find that the process of settling your husband's estate will yield many small wins for you. Each private little accomplishment as you work through the process sets you on the track to build your confidence and prepares you for developing the next phase of your family's legacy plan.

Create the Next Phase of Your Family's Legacy Plan

As you settle his estate and accept responsibility for the future direction of your family, you will have a broader understanding of your family's situation and your choices. You can use the momentum that you and your husband created to keep your family going in roughly the same direction. You can choose to alter it slightly. Or you can take your family in a radically new direction. It is up to you, because you are now in a position that calls for developing a new life plan.

It takes a lot of pressure off people to know that every couple has three stories—his story, her story, and their story. During their lives together it helps them to respect and support each other on individual issues and collaborate on others.

But you, as a widow, now have a new perspective and new opportunities. As long as you abide by the restrictions of the will and trust, it's like your life ahead is a clean sheet of paper. You have the opportunity to retain the status quo, reconfigure things, or reinvent yourself. Maybe something did not work in the old compromise, so you have a pent-up desire to try something new.

Nanette's Story

Nanette provides a simple example. After her husband died, she immediately sold his SUV and bought a luxury sedan. She explained, "He loved that SUV. I didn't."

I recall a more complex example from a couple in a second marriage that had children from the first marriages. When he died, the families came to immediate odds over who was to get what.

Pam's Story

Pam's first husband had very little when she met him. They had three kids and then divorced. The second husband, also a divorcé with children, came along and didn't have much money either. While they were married, Pam supported her second husband, kept him going, and then helped him manage a significant inheritance from his mother. When he passed away, his trust named her as trustee and income beneficiary, and his children from the previous marriage as remainder beneficiaries.

She had use of the assets to produce income for her during her lifetime. But at her passing, his kids were designated to get what was left. She felt his kids didn't like her because she was a second wife. She, naturally, wanted to take care of her kids. So her "job," as far as she was concerned, was to distribute as much as possible from the trust—and transfer it to them.

Her lawyer had to remind her that legally, as trustee, she was responsible to two sets of beneficiaries. She was responsible to herself as the income beneficiary. She was also responsible to her husband's kids as the remainder beneficiaries. As trustee, she also had to account to all of the beneficiaries every year as to what she did with the assets of the trust. The beneficiaries then had 30 days to object to the accounting. And, by the way, if she didn't account to them, her husband's kids could have her removed as trustee. So, instead of being the trustee and in control, she would be at the mercy of his children. Pam quickly learned how to perform her fiduciary responsibilities as trustee.

Your Advisory Team—
Your Three-Legged Step Stool to the Future

Complex problems, like the one I just described, will be challenging to handle as you work to become self-sufficient, settle your husband's estate, and prepare a new legacy plan. But remember that you have much strength to draw on. These include your faith, the values expressed in your family financial philosophy, the genuine support from family and friends, your lifetime of momentum, your trusted advisor, and this book. Plus there are other resources available to you to get the job done.

As a surviving spouse gains clarity during our initial meeting, I like to explain to her that she can and should draw on expert help from other advisors as well.

I suggest envisioning this core team of specialists as a three-legged stool. The widow is stepping on the stool as she reaches for the future. The platform is the planning that gives you the framework for moving forward. This is typically done with your trusted advisor holding your hand. The three legs—tax, legal, and investment specialists—support the stool. In our office, we often fill two roles. As a planner, I coordinate the team to work toward the client's vision of the future. At the same time, our firm can also fill the role of investment advisor, an essential leg of the stool.

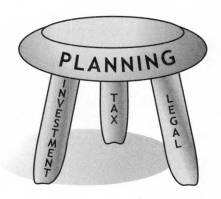

YOUR THREE-LEGGED STEP STOOL TO THE FUTURE

The team selection depends on your family's needs and existing relationships between you and the specialists. The important thing is to pull together a team and decide who will do what. Each team member will apply special knowledge to issues that come up to give you the best alternative strategies.

Getting each team member's perspective becomes especially valuable. As you determine investment policy and invest assets within the estate settlement trusts, there are always many possible combinations of solutions with legal, tax, and investment implications. Your trusted advisor can act as the team center point. In that position, he can help coordinate all the information and options available to you and work with you on making prudent decisions.

CHAPTER FIVE

Stabilize Step 2— Renewal of Confidence

As is our confidence, so is our capacity.

—William Hazlitt

Now that you have begun dealing with tasks common to every widow, it's time to address the issues that apply specifically to you. Once you identify and begin working with your team, remember the three-legged stool as you progress through this second step of the stabilization phase.

Your team will help you look ahead as you become more emotionally and financially stable. Regaining both kinds of stability will increase your confidence to move on. Though your team will outline many tasks and deadlines, your trusted advisor ideally will help you break each down into finite, eminently doable pieces.

Identify Your Team

During your first meeting, you and your trusted advisor talked about why you need a team. No matter how comfortable you feel with your advisor, it's in your best interests to accept the interdependence of a team. As you probably know, interdependence is when independent individuals work together so the results of their efforts are greater than the sum of each one's work.

Acknowledge the Complexities You Face

Your trusted advisor can act as your advocate and center point to gather and evaluate many kinds of information. But it makes legal, financial, and emotional sense to draw on the expertise of those who know most about specific issues such as cash flow planning, portfolio integrity, business valuation, trust funding and distribution rules, fiduciary responsibilities, trust design, and other seemingly esoteric topics.

As an example, estate planning lawyer Paul McEwen explains, "I have specific knowledge of a broad variety of trusts, but it's not necessary for me to explain each specific option for each client. It makes more sense for a planner, like Buddy Thomas, to lead that discussion. He understands the client's big-picture vision and goals. Together we can figure out which kind of trust will best help a surviving spouse fill obligations to beneficiaries—especially when there are two sets of children from different marriages. Then, when the client has chosen a trust type, I can very effectively draft the legal documents."

Meanwhile, Paul McEwen and I often look to CPA Jim Perich, who specializes in estate settlement, trust accounting, and taxation. Jim understands tax consequences and knows how to work with the IRS to resolve many kinds of estate tax disputes. His immense knowledge, insight, and wisdom make him a vital member of the team.

Choose the Team That Best Fits You

You now have an idea of the positions you need to fill to create a team that will serve you best. This is the time to act on the difference between your story as a couple and your individual story. In other words, say your husband always worked with the same accountant for years. They golfed together. They liked each other. Don't rule out the value of your husband's insights. But know it is now your job and your team. Only you will be responsible for the outcome, so it is perfectly okay for you to exercise your own choice. You will be working with your team for at least two years and probably longer, so feel free to choose people according to what works best for you.

If you know what you want and do not want, then you know what to look for when you interview candidates to replace someone. You may want to use the exercise in Chapter Two. Knowing that there is a team, knowing which seats have to be filled, taking an inventory of who has to do what, knowing you have an estate settlement track to run on—all enhance confidence.

Your Financial and Emotional Stability

It is not easy to become self sufficient, settle an estate and develop a new plan when you are grieving. Yet, if you deal with each of these five major tasks a little at a time, you will not only regain but also build new financial and emotional stability. Even when you feel emotionally vulnerable, you can manage these next steps—because each is finite and has a deadline.

If It Doesn't Feel Right, Check It Out

Marcia's case offers an excellent example of how you can take steps towards financial stability, even while your emotions are raw. At her husband's funeral, she told me, "I just have a feeling that you and I should talk." So we set an appointment.

Marcia's Story

When Marcia came in, she told me she had gone to her family lawyer and asked, "What do I do now?" He told her, "You don't have to do anything. You're done. You have a trust, so you're all set." Actually, this could have been grounds for malpractice. If Marcia had done nothing, she would not have funded the trusts called for in the family's living trust. And taking no action literally nullifies all the planning.

Most lawyers who do estate planning also do estate settlement. For some reason, Marcia's lawyer only did estate planning. So it is fortunate she questioned his answer. Actually, she would rather have accepted the lawyer's advice. Like many widows, she was shocked to find out that after a spouse dies you have to inventory and appraise all the business and personal assets. She said, "This seems like an awful lot of work!" But we helped her every step of the way to comply with her role as trustee.

The original plan, a good one, had to be implemented. Marcia now understands it and makes decisions with confidence and an eye toward the future. She often admits she is learning all the time.

Ellen's Story

Another widow, Ellen, came to me completely distraught. When she and her husband were in their late 60s, I had helped them set up an insured retirement plan. They had used most of their money to put their three kids through medical, law, and business schools. Her husband was an entrepreneur, several times just missing his big payoff. When he died, Ellen knew there wasn't a lot of income-producing assets to work with.

But with the team cooperating, including her kids, she found a way to make it work. After significant thought and prayer, she chose to move from the West Coast to the Midwest, but on her own terms. She is near her family now and has a new career—in her seventies. She absolutely loves her choices and is confident about her future.

Deal With Your Particulars

As I have mentioned, one key to financial and emotional stability is to figure out how much money you need to live on for the next six months to a year. Cutting through this uncertainty—and planning for interim cash flow—provides an unbelievable amount of confidence.

I recently got a call from a friend whose sister's spouse had been a prominent businessman on the East Coast. My friend told me, "My brother-in-law was making good money and they spent much of it on their lifestyle. Their assets are not even close to producing enough income to support that lifestyle. Yet there is no doubt in my mind that she will be able to handle the adjustment and take control within a couple of years—as long as someone teaches her how."

As we have done with so many other surviving spouses, we drew up a plan to identify income-producing assets, such as bank accounts and life insurance. We defined what adjustments the widow would have to make initially. We earmarked enough to get her through two years, and now we are helping her plan for what will happen next.

You and your team will completely assess your specific situation, leaving no issue unattended. Your starter check list will be similar to the following:

1. Plan time to grieve.
2. Identify your trusted advisor (may or may not be team leader).
3. Determine six months to a year monthly income need for your desired lifestyle (including entertainment, travel, and gifting).
4. Identify source of monthly income.
5. Inventory all assets/liabilities.
6. Identify other advisors that will complete your three-legged stool.
7. Obtain copies of death certificates.
8. Notify all institutions of spouse's death.
9. Calculate estate tax day: date of death (DOD) plus nine months.
10. Calculate trust funding day: date of death (DOD) plus approximately one year.
11. Open probate if necessary.

When you have addressed these items, you will be ready for the third and final step of the stabilization phase— determining your priorities.

CHAPTER SIX

Stabilize Step 3—
Determine Your Priorities

You can't teach a kid to ride a bike at a seminar.

— David Sandler

By now you have begun dealing with tasks common to every widow. You have identified your team, and together, you have assessed your specific situation. Good work! You are now ready for the third and final step of the stabilization phase—determining your priorities.

The chapter you are reading will give you a visual map of your essential tasks for the next two years or so. It also describes how to deal with your grief in a way that will help you say, on the first anniversary of your husband's death, "I have used this year well. I understand and have applied the Widow's Bridge® method to this difficult transition in my life, and I'm confident that I have built a good base for future decisions."

Visualize Your Tasks

As you begin to list all your legal and fiduciary responsibilities, you may be tempted to reach for perfection. Does that sound like you? If so, please stop. Take a deep breath. Don't set yourself up for this disappointment. No one is perfect. Just think of all the rockets that rocket scientists blew up before they put a man on the moon. It's true that you and your team have a lot to do. But—other than making sure you fulfill "must do" tasks in time, such as filing the estate tax return—you should feel free to modify and alter your master plan as you go.

What's more important is having a good overall understanding of where your five major tasks will fit into the first two years after your husband's death. For this we recommend studying the following chart and setting up a simple filing system.

Use a Timeline

This chart gives you a visual map of the five categories of transition activities that surviving spouses must deal with: grieve, manage your lifestyle cash flow, manage your investment portfolio, settle your spouse's estate, and develop the next variation of your family legacy plan (phase two).

FIVE CATEGORIES OF TRANSITION ACTIVITIES FOR WIDOWS(ERS)

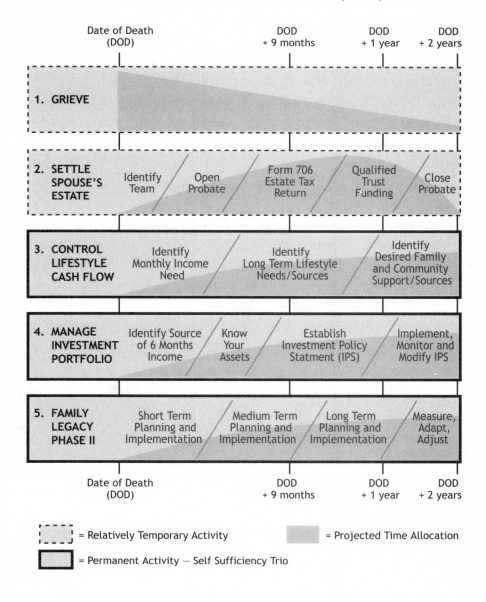

Set Up a Five-File System

You will be dealing with many kinds of documents over the next two years. Setting up five files (one for each of the five categories) will help you bring order out of potential chaos. Choose what works best for you, perhaps a filing cabinet drawer or section for each category.

For example, people may give you books and written prayers about grieving; you may want to respond to some of these gifts. You might find it helpful to file these resources, along with appropriate stationery, in a drawer marked Grieving.

Documents about what you have, want, and need go in your Lifestyle Cash Flow and Portfolio Management drawer. Sort other paperwork into your Estate Settlement drawer. Within these categories, you can easily create subsets, including Pending and Completed items. Eventually you'll need only three files—two for Self-Sufficiency (which includes Lifestyle Income and Expenses, and Investment Portfolio) and one for Family Legacy Planning. As you glimpse into your future and move on, you will be able to close your Estate Settlement file and eventually your Grieving file.

Make Grief Work for You

Grieving takes precedence among your five tasks. If you feel like you have to grieve, then do it. In *On Your Own*, authors Alexandra Armstrong (a financial planner) and Mary R. Donahue (a widow) say that the way you respond to your husband's death will depend on how you personally experience grief; specific circumstances, such as how well your husband provided for you; and whether your marriage was harmonious.

No matter how these factors influence your bereavement, you need to seek support. Your trusted advisor and your team will help you toward greater emotional and financial stability. Authors Armstrong and Donahue encourage widows to not worry about "imposing on" family or friends. "Friends, by definition, are there for both the good and bad times," they say. Like other widows, you may also find comfort in making new friends among other widows or talking with your doctor, spiritual counselor, or trusted advisor.

Grieving is important. But you don't want to devote every minute to it. To divert your attention from grieving for a while, pick up the estate settlement process.

Soon after her husband died, I asked Gretchen, an executive with a defense contractor, "How are you doing?" She replied, "Sometimes really good, sometimes not so good. There are days I bury myself in work to divert myself from how bad I feel. Other times I sit and cry. Sometimes I read literature on the investments my advisor suggests I use to fund the trusts. At times I go out with friends or family to maintain a social life. And sometimes all I want to do is work away on details of settling the estate."

Every time we talked, Gretchen felt a little better. Six months after her husband's death, she bought a car, using an account her husband had set up in trust with money inherited from his mother. "That's just like him. He's still taking care of me," she said.

Slow But Steady

In the first year after your husband's death, you and your team will spend a lot of time on the details of settling his estate. This includes probating the will, inventorying the assets, funding the trusts and dealing with a tidal wave of paperwork.

In a Pittsburgh estate lawyer's office, I recall seeing a coffee-table book that detailed the wills of our American presidents. George Washington's will directed that his slaves be set free. Franklin D. Roosevelt's will requested that Eleanor either sell his extensive naval history collection or give all the books, prints, and manuscripts to one of their children. But the page for John F. Kennedy simply said, "President Kennedy died with his estate in trust."

A will is public—sort of like a probate judge dumping out the contents of a briefcase for all to see. A trust is private, with the trustee removing things one by one from the briefcase and passing out each piece so only the recipient sees it.

Hopefully all your major assets are already in trust, so that your husband's will deals only with where a few remaining things should go. If not, the probate process must determine that his will is, in fact, his last testament and accurately states his intentions. The court is then responsible to oversee the process of distribution. If your husband died intestate (without a will), then the laws of your state will grind the estate through a tedious, public, expensive probate. And those laws will dictate who gets what, based on your family's configuration at the time of your husband's death. If you are lucky, probate will last only eighteen months.

The average widow we work with is surprised to find she must inventory and appraise all the business and personal assets her husband owned on the date of his death. But she feels relieved to learn that our team will help gather statements and assist her in communicating with all the people who were involved in the family finances. Jim Perich, the CPA we often work with, says, "Widows usually call me quite a bit with questions during this process. We need to establish the asset inventory so we can prepare federal and state tax returns." You will recall from previous chapters that the IRS Form 706 estate tax return must be filed within nine months of your husband's death.

If you have a living trust, then inventorying your husband's estate prepares you to meet your legal responsibilities as trustee, which are quite strict. The estate planning lawyer on your team will assist you with the legal aspects of this process, usually during the first year. Your trusted advisor and others on your team will help you write investment policies for identifying and moving assets into the various trusts.

Settling the estate also requires handling hundreds of pieces of paper. Our client Nanette had known for a year that her husband was dying of cancer. She and her husband were very efficient and prepared everything they could before his death. Yet she still had a ton of paperwork after his death. Like your husband probably was, hers was on scores of mailing lists—from junk mail and magazine subscriptions to bank statements, insurance premiums, and auto registrations. It took her over a year to weed through medical bills. And widows must also check whether their husband's death makes them eligible for benefits from his employer, the military, the government, credit card companies, or membership associations.

Efficient even after her husband's death, Nanette told me, "I have waves of paperwork every week in the mail box. I decided I had to do at least one complete task every day. I could pick from the top or bottom of the pile or wait till I got a third notice on a bill. Even if you take care of just one piece of paper per day, you can get an amazing amount of work done."

Using the Year Well

If you follow the prioritizing suggestions listed above, you will be able to look back with satisfaction on your first year as a widow. Chances are you will have chiseled many chips from your boulder of grief. You will have experienced increased confidence in your ability to operate as the sole financial head of your family. And you will have made substantial progress in settling the estate.

During your first year as a widow, you and your team will also begin talking about—and with some short- and medium-term issues, implementing changes that will affect your future. All this prepares you to enter the next phase of the Widow's Bridge®—planning—which in itself, among other things, creates a tremendous sense of empowerment.

CHAPTER SEVEN

Plan Step 4 — Empowerment

*It's easy to say "no"
when there is a deeper "yes"
burning inside.*

— Stephen R. Covey

By now, three to six months have passed since your husband's death. You have experienced or at least understand most of your responsibilities, and you're probably feeling some comfort in working with your trusted advisor. You are now entering the planning phase, the second of three main phases that make the Widow's Bridge® a healthy transition process. The planning phase has three steps, and this chapter deals with empowerment, that next logical step to move forward.

You'll remember that your entire two-year transition period involves eight steps. That means that when you address the elements described in this chapter on empowerment, you will be halfway through the process—looking to the horizon of your new life.

The first phase, stabilization, often takes up to six months, or more. The second phase, planning, can be accomplished over the next six to nine months. The third phase of initial transition, implementation, can run approximately nine to twelve months. All of these time frames are estimates based on our experiences. As you get comfortable with the process, you will naturally know when to give yourself more time and when to move on.

Are you starting to feel more clear about how you'll survive your husband's death and more confident that you can make a new life for yourself? This clarity and confidence mark the beginning of your emerging empowerment, the process of digging down inside yourself to find the courage and strength to move forward definitively.

Running throughout this book are the strong spans of the bridge that support you during your darkest hours as you cross over to a brighter future. At this moment, just know it can be done. Widows' new lives are works in progress. You are making the transition from surviving spouse to family matriarch. But only you can do it your way.

Just like the butterfly, only you can break through your cocoon. And it is in your struggle that you will find and renew the strength that will empower you to do what must be done now and in the future to take charge of your new life.

Though your trusted advisor is a helping hand, the decisions must be yours. For it is the exercise of making decisions and living with them that will make you strong and give you the experience to develop your own unique wisdom that you can build upon the rest of your life.

Now is the time to find a way to gain perspective on all the issues you will face as you move into the planning phase. Financial planning requires you to address issues for *today and tomorrow*. We have found an effective way to organize your decisions by labeling each issue as one of three categories: *Lifestyle, Portfolio,* or *Legacy.* Then, further prioritizing each issue by whether it must be acted on today or in the future. You will have a balanced approach to your future financial success when you take into consideration all three categories of your wealth management as well as the issues of *Today* and the *Future* for each. This gives you a total of six areas to consider simultaneously. The Superplan® Model, located on the next page, has been used successfully in keeping all six areas in perspective.

The Superplan® Matrix on the following page can be used to maintain perspective as you *focus-decide-act* on each issue while also considering the other five.

THE KEY TO A SUCCESSFUL FINANCIAL FUTURE

Addressing Today's Issues with an Eye on Tomorrow

SUPERPLAN® MODEL		
LIFESTYLE CASHFLOW FUTURE	**PORTFOLIO INTEGRITY FUTURE**	**LEGACY IMPACT FUTURE**
LIFESTYLE CASHFLOW *TODAY*	**PORTFOLIO INTEGRITY** *TODAY*	**LEGACY IMPACT** *TODAY*

TIME ↑

| LIFESTYLE CASHFLOW | PORTFOLIO INTEGRITY | LEGACY IMPACT |

————————— PRIORITY —————————→

The three basic elements of wealth management are addressed in their order of priority and with regards to the future consequences of today's decisions.

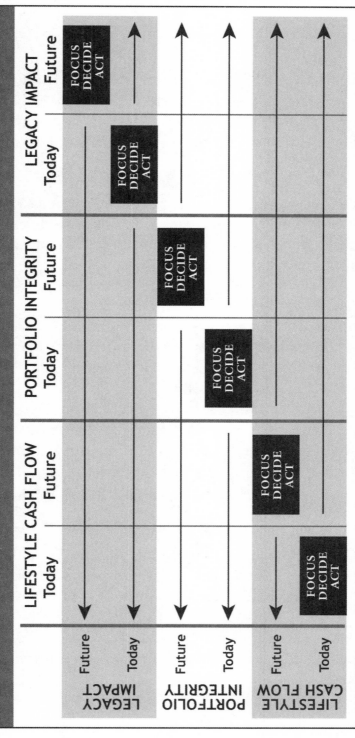

SUPERPLAN® MATRIX

As each issue is addressed, the other five are taken into consideration in order to make balanced decisions.

The Superplan® approach may sound complicated because as you address each issue, it is important to think about how that decision will affect all the others. However, it is a common sense process that can help you decide what is most important to you and help you focus on getting things done.

With your team's help, you have inventoried what you have and detailed how much it costs to live. You've stabilized your financial situation and identified your initial income sources. This stability lets you look to the horizon for a better tomorrow. Whether you have the assets of Mother Theresa or Bill Gates, financial transcendence is possible once you know exactly how much it costs you to live and how much is available.

Now it's time to think about the financial assets you actually have to work with... or not... as you create your future. Facing these facts and understanding your portfolio may sound scary, but as our clients have discovered, confronting and dealing with your financial fears is more empowering than ignoring or trying not to worry about them.

Your task is to accept that, like the sign in the mall states, "You are here." Your trusted advisor's job is to make that "map of the mall" as broad and as clear as possible.

One way to establish your present situation is to follow the simple "Financial Empowerment Exercise" on the following page.

Know Your Assets

Financial Empowerment Exercise

1. List all of your assets in the following 3 categories:
- *Portfolio* (passive investments that can or do produce income)
- *Business* (direct or active ownership of closely-held businesses or income-producing real estate)
- *Use* (homes, boats, cars, collectibles, etc.)

2. Attach a liquidation value (the price you could sell the asset for in the next 30 days) to your **portfolio** assets and multiply the total by .003.

3. Enter the amount of monthly income you can reasonably expect from your **business** and other sources (employment, social security, pensions, etc.).

4. Now, combine your total portfolio income (#2) and total other monthly income (#3).

This is your maximum potential monthly income. Though oversimplified, this formula is designed to give you a sense of how much money could be available per month, indefinitely. If your monthly income is less than your monthy expenses, you have two choices: reduce expenses, sell a use asset or assets to invest and generate more income, or both.

Ginny's Story

This was certainly true in our dealings with Ginny, a widow who sensed she was living beyond her means. Her adult children were hanging around—exacerbating the problem. One son kept putting Ginny's money into losing businesses. Another son was on drugs. One daughter was using family money to support her boyfriends.

Ginny was sick with stress. She developed stress-related ailments and was disintegrating before our eyes. Our team laid out the long-term asset identification process for her. We listed all potential resources and explained, "Ginny, if you had all these assets and they were producing income, here's how much you'd get a month."

She realized that her home—her husband's trophy house—was a significant part of her asset base. Yet she was still paying a mortgage on it, rather than receiving an income from it. Facing facts about her assets helped Ginny make an important decision. She decided to go house shopping.

Restate Your Vision

Ginny saw that the time had come to restate her values, which helped her clarify her financial vision. Her advisory team then faced the challenge of helping her spell out a long-term investment policy based on that new vision.

During the stabilization phase, we had eliminated many of the economic dangers Ginny feared immediately after her husband's death. However, we all recognized that Ginny could still lose her independence, income, or ability to help her loved ones unless she managed her assets in accordance with what really mattered to her. That is why we advise a surviving spouse to err on the conservative side.

Ginny loved her children and wanted the best for them. In the short term, letting her adult children live with her seemed like something a loving mother would do. But Ginny admitted to herself that she was actually enabling her adult children to continue their bad habits. Besides, doing the "Financial Empowerment" exercise revealed that she could not afford to keep living in her large home. The whole family would suffer—emotionally and financially.

So Ginny decided to look for a smaller home with room only for herself and one responsible daughter. The other children would have no choice but to move on and take charge of their lives. Making this decision changed Ginny's life. She lost weight and became healthier and happier.

Frankly, Ginny is not the only client who had to prod adult children to become more responsible. We have seen the same situation in other families. Parents who have the means to help their children think they should do so. Isn't that the most loving choice? Maybe not. As one client put it, "Large gifts never seem to have the effect you think they will. Maybe it's better to not make outright gifts to anyone."

Reach for a "Deeper Yes"

Thoroughly understanding the assets for her financial future and using them in accordance with her values helped Ginny take her first steps into empowerment. This freed her to feel good about doing things for herself, rather than channeling all her resources to her children—who would be better off anyway by earning their own keep. Because she chose "taking care of myself" as one of her restated values, Ginny made sure her long-term financial plan included money set aside for a yearly cruise.

In his classic book *The Seven Habits of Highly Effective People,* Stephen R. Covey explains that people often let urgent matters crowd out important ones. Urgent matters, he says, "press on us; they insist on action. They are often popular with others." Important issues are often less visible, yet they contribute "to your mission, your values, your high priority goals." Important issues lead to results, but those results won't happen unless we take action.

In Ginny's case, her adult children were pressing her for money. Giving them what they wanted kept her in their good graces. But to truly act as the sole head of her family, Ginny had to look beyond her children's urgent demands to address what was more important—what would be best for her family over the long run.

As Covey states and restates in several ways throughout his books, "It's almost impossible to say 'no' if you don't have a bigger 'yes' burning inside." Ginny had a deeper "yes."

Developing the courage to restate and act on her financial values gave Ginny a baseline for creating a new life plan. Her decisions put her on firm ground for the future. This firm ground was the right setting for our three-legged stool. Stepping onto the stool reminded Ginny that she now had a general direction for a plan. She noticed more opportunities each day, knew her team would help her evaluate each option, and began to believe that her dreams and desires were truly attainable.

By now, I hope you share some of that same confidence. If so, you are ready to take control, ready to take the next step of the planning phase—constructing a vision.

CHAPTER EIGHT

Plan Step 5—
Planning for Tomorrow/
Constructing a Vision
of the Future

*Vision controls our perception,
and our perception becomes our reality.*

— Dewitt Jones

Some widows can focus on the future sooner than others. Only you will know when you are ready. Most start to think about it around six months after their spouse's death. You will know when you are ready when you have stabilized your finances, stopped the downward spiral of emotions, and are beginning to feel empowered to start building a new life. In other words, you have left a bad road and turned onto what could be a wonderful main highway.

This is the middle of the planning phase, the second of three main phases of the Widow's Bridge®. The planning phase has three steps, and this chapter deals with constructing a vision, the second planning step.

Instead of constantly thinking back to what was, you are anchored in the present and ready to envision a future. In his video "Celebrate What's Right with the World," former *National Geographic* photographer Dewitt Jones acknowledges that change frightens many of us. He also says that no matter "how bleak, dry, desolate, or devoid of possibility" your situation seems, the "times of most change always hold the most potential." The following exercise will help you build a vision of possibility, not scarcity. You will brainstorm with those closest to you about what you want for yourself and quantify what you'll need to do.

Focus on the Future You Want

Before we specifically help you focus on the future you want for yourself, let me offer a context that our clients find helpful.

The River and the Wheel: We often help clients visualize what is ahead by talking about what we call "the river of family financial growth." The river flows through the stages of financial dependence, independence, and transcendence.

THE RIVER OF FAMILY FINANCIAL GROWTH

Like almost everyone else in our society, you started out in financial dependence. First we are dependent on our parents, then on our jobs. Our firm helps clients plan wisely so that their assets eventually generate enough passive income for them to graduate into the state of financial independence. At this stage you don't have to work for your money, because your money works for you. From this very secure position, people begin to think about financial transcendence—the process of moving beyond a focus on financial security to creating a legacy. With confidence in their position, they focus, decide, and act on how they will give back to the world while living a confident lifestyle.

Underneath the river of financial growth are potential earthquakes, like death, disability, divorce, significant financial losses, and liens from would-be creditors. Above the river there is a sun, which represents life's positive events, like a new baby, new marriage, or significant financial gain.

Financial planners, investment advisors, insurance agents, lawyers, and accountants have been helping people plan for or clean up after these events as a matter of course, for as long as they have been around.

Since these events usually happen randomly, with no two families experiencing the same number, occurrence, or sequence, it is difficult to characterize them as a group and even more difficult to plan for them.

One approach that has worked for us is to think of these random events in four categories:

- Turning the Page
  (the sale of a business, career change, or career exit)

- New Life
  (a marriage, a birth, or starting a new business)

- The Dastardly Ds
  (death, divorce, disability, or other disaster)

- Big Money Matters
  (a significant economic gain or loss or lien
  by creditor)

Quantified all together, we call this the "life event big spin wheel." You never know which of these things will happen to you or when any of them will happen. But it is extremely helpful to know that one of these events may, and probably will, happen as you reach for your own vision. This framework also helps you prepare for how you might deal with wherever you land on the life-event big spin wheel. Visualizing the river and wheel helps us talk with clients about these specific dangers and opportunities. It lets us prepare for and plan for consequences.

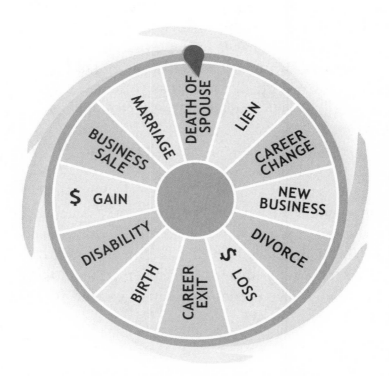

THE LIFE-EVENT BIG-SPIN WHEEL

Brainstorming Your Possible Futures

Now let's move from the general context to you, specifically. Certainly you have experienced one of life's "dastardly Ds"—the upheaval of your husband's death. Please take a minute to also think about and describe where you are in the financial growth river.

Whether you see yourself in a state of financial dependence, independence, or transcendence, it's time to focus on your future. You might ask a friend, a family member, a support group, or your trusted advisor to facilitate by helping you brainstorm the following exercise based on Dan Sullivan's *R-Factor Question*. Remember that brainstorming simply means listing possibilities. Don't censor or second-guess yourself as you answer these questions. Don't stop to consider whether all your answers are consistent. Rather, just record what flows out of your heart and mouth. In fact, you might ask them to jot down key phrases for you.

Imagine yourself one year from now, on a lunch date with an old friend you haven't seen since your spouse passed away. You've built as happy a life as you could imagine since then. Now you and your friend are looking back on how far you've come, and you're excited to tell them the news.

Here's the question: What would have had to have happened during that time for you to feel you had made the kind of progress you imagined?

Take some time to apply this question to each aspect of your life:

- What about your lifestyle did you maintain or change so that, a year later, you feel you've made progress?
- Did you and your husband start something that you are finishing?
- What did you learn, join, achieve, experience, visit, or make?
- Did you have more income and feel comfortable with the source?
- Think about your portfolio. Are you happy simply with a fixed income, or did you feel a need to invest more aggressively for the future you desire?

Be optimistic, but realistic, and as specific as you can.

Another Perspective

Now let's pretend something completely different. Imagine you passed away yesterday.

- Who did you help?
- What would have happened with this wealth?
- What would you have wanted to happen?

Answering these questions will give you perspective to imagine the kind of legacy you want to and can create.

As you work through these exercises, pay attention to two threads in your answers. Some aspects of your answers will be strictly logical or intellectual. Yet you'll probably feel somewhat emotional in considering other facets. For example, you might say, "I just *want* to keep our house!" (an emotional response). Logically, you might ask yourself to *think* (an intellectual response) about what would be different if you couldn't keep the house.

From Brainstorm to Future Focus

With your facilitator's help, summarize the discussion you've just had about your future. Work from the master list you just created during your brainstorm session. Use a word or two to describe each idea you came up with, and note whether it's more an emotional or intellectual idea.

As an example the following chart was completed by a widow who had these feelings about her lifestyle: "I want to live the way I choose." "I want to be able to support myself." Her feelings also sparked specific thoughts: "I need to know my options." "I need to live within my means."

Following her example, fill in at least two thoughts and feelings for your lifestyle, portfolio, and legacy in the blank worksheet provided on the page following.

Note: Print-ready Superplan® forms can be obtained from www.widowsbridge.com

SUPERPLAN® FUTURE FOCUS WORKSHEET

	EMOTIONAL (I Feel)	INTELLECTUAL (I Think)	SMART (Goal)
LIFESTYLE	• •	• •	• •
PORTFOLIO	• •	• •	• •
LEGACY	• •	• •	• •

Print-ready Superplan® forms can be obtained from www.widowsbridge.com

SUPERPLAN® FUTURE FOCUS WORKSHEET

	EMOTIONAL (I Feel)	INTELLECTUAL (I Think)	SMART GOAL
LIFESTYLE	• I want to live the way I choose. • I want to be able to support myself.	• I need to know my options. • I need to live within my means.	
PORTFOLIO	• I want to be in control of my wealth. • I want to know if I am making financial progress or not.	• It's important to understand my finances. • How will I know if I'm doing ok?	
LEGACY	• I want to take care of my family and help my favorite charity. • I want to know my affairs are in order if I should pass away.	• How much is enough? Too much? • I know it gets complicated and expensive for heirs.	

From Future Focus to SMART Goals

A very important step of this three-part Superplan®
Future Focus worksheet is to fill in the SMART goal
column. SMART is an acronym for:

- **S**PECIFIC
- **M**EASURABLE
- **A**CHIEVABLE
- **R**EALISTIC
- **T**IMELY

We ask you to write out SMART goals because these characteristics distinguish a goal from a dream. A basic plan
will have at least two goals in each of the three categories:
Lifestyle, Portfolio, and *Legacy.*

In our widow's example on the next page, evaluating the emotional and logical strands of her thoughts about *Lifestyle, Portfolio,* and *Legacy* led her to two SMART goals (Specific, Measurable, Achievable, Realistic, Timely) in each of the three categories. For example in the *Lifestyle* category, she decided to maintain her current standard of living indefinitely. She also decided to make a goal to take two weeks of vacation every quarter, beginning that quarter.

Follow the example of *Portfolio* and *Legacy* goals to get a further understanding of the Superplan® goal setting process.

SUPERPLAN® FUTURE FOCUS WORKSHEET

	EMOTIONAL (I Feel)	INTELLECTUAL (I Think)	SMART GOAL
LIFESTYLE	• I want to live the way I choose. • I want to be able to support myself.	• I need to know my options. • I need to live within my means.	• Maintain my current standard of living indefinitely. • Take two weeks vacation every quarter beginning this quarter.
PORTFOLIO	• I want to be in control of my wealth. • I want to know if I am making financial progress or not.	• It's important to understand my finances. • How will I know if I'm doing ok?	• Take control of the family wealth (within 60 days). • Monitor my financial progress against milestones at least semi-annually.
LEGACY	• I want to take care of my family and help my favorite charity. • I want to know my affairs are in order if I should pass away.	• How much is enough? Too much? • I know it gets complicated and expensive for heirs.	• Arrange my affairs for lifetime giving as I choose (within 180 days). • Arrange my affairs for distribution at my death in line with my desires (within 1 year).

Now, working with your trusted advisor, fill in your SMART goals in your blank Superplan® Future Focus worksheet (four pages back). List your most important goals for the Lifestyle, Portfolio, and Legacy you envision.

Refine and Prioritize

Once you've filled in your worksheet, you'll see you have six general categories that describe parts of your possible future. Some of the items may seem to contradict each other. Taken together, they may seem like they represent more than any one person could follow through and manage.

But that's natural. When you look at multiple goals simultaneously, they can seem to counteract each other. However, when you act on them individually giving consideration to the rest, you enhance your ability to reach them all.

The exercise you just completed marks the beginning of your plan for your future. It is the glimmer of light that, with time, patience, and nurturing, has vast potential to shine brightly on the possibilities ahead. The Superplan® Future Focus worksheet summarizes the foundation of your future as you choose which possibilities to act on.

Now that you have addressed your personal wants and desires, it's time to develop the strategies to achieve them. Remember the sequence. *Focus* on each issue. *Decide* on your best alternative. *Act* on your decision.

Does envisioning your possible future make you feel a little more in control than when you began this chapter? If so, then you are ready to move on to the final step of the planning phase—creating your new strategy.

CHAPTER NINE

Plan Step 6—
Your "New" Strategy

You've got to make a conscious choice every day to shed the old—whatever "the old" means for you.

— Sarah Ban Breathnach

Do you have the sense that things are beginning to happen? As you psychologically take control of your future, some of your dreams are coming into focus as real goals. These indicators show that you are ready to chart your new course. Now is the time to create your new strategy. The new foundation you have put in place since your husband died has positioned you to choose your best path to take as you reach for your new future.

This chapter is designed to help you determine what you need to do to get from where you are now to where you want to be. You'll decide on your strategic plan. You'll also experience a bonus, that will be revealed later, while working through this goal-cultivating exercise.

The Situation Dictates Your Strategy

Pull out the completed Superplan® Future Focus worksheet you developed while working through the last chapter. The difference between where you are and where you want to be will help you find your strategy. We like to say that "the situation dictates the solution." Following the Superplan® process will help you clarify your present situation to help you dictate your best alternative solution.

Transfer Your SMART Goals

The next tool is the Superplan® Strategic Decision worksheet; see illustration on the next page.

SUPERPLAN® STRATEGY DECISION WORKSHEET

LIFESTYLE	SMART GOAL (Restated)	PRESENT SITUATION	STRATEGY
LIFESTYLE			
PORTFOLIO			
LEGACY			

Print-ready Superplan® forms can be obtained from www.widowsbridge.com

In the example illustration, located on the next page, the SMART goals will look familiar. That's because you last saw them as the third column of the example widow's completed Superplan® Future Focus worksheet.

So you already have a head start. Simply transfer your SMART goals into the blank worksheet from Superplan® Future Focus worksheet. Be sure to refine them if you neglected one of the five essential SMART characteristics the first time you wrote out your goals. List at least two goals per category.

SUPERPLAN® STRATEGY DECISION WORKSHEET

	SMART GOAL (Restated)	PRESENT SITUATION	STRATEGY
LIFESTYLE	• Maintain my current standard of living indefinitely. • Take two weeks vacation every quarter beginning this quarter.		
PORTFOLIO	• Take control of the family wealth (within 60 days). • Monitor my financial progress at least semi-annually.		
LEGACY	• Arrange my affairs for lifetime giving as I choose (within 180 days). • Arrange my affairs for distribution at my death in line with my desires (within 1 year).		

Describe Your Present Situation

Now, following the example illustration located on the next page, for each of your six goals, make a present position statement. In the *Lifestyle* category, our widow made it her goal to maintain her current standard of living for the foreseeable future. But when she wrote that goal, she admitted to herself that, although she had a general idea of her monthly *Lifestyle* income need, she was not sure how to support it indefinitely.

In her *Portfolio* category, one of her goals was to take control of the family wealth within 60 days. However, her reality was that her husband had handled the finances, so she had only a vague idea of how he controlled the family wealth.

Brainstorm Alternative Strategies

The example illustration, located on the page following, lists only one strategy per goal in the third column. But now that you have established where you are with respect to where you want to be, you and your trusted advisor can brainstorm several alternative strategies for reaching your goals. We call it the "what if" game.

You may be getting a sense of how difficult this would be to do alone. However, with the help of your trusted advisor, know that it is eminently doable.

SUPERPLAN® STRATEGY DECISION WORKSHEET

	SMART GOAL (*Restated*)	PRESENT SITUATION	STRATEGY
LIFESTYLE	• Maintain my current standard of living indefinitely. • Take two weeks vacation every quarter beginning this quarter.	• I have a general idea of my monthly lifestyle need but am not sure how I can support it. • Travel money can be taken as needed from savings.	
PORTFOLIO	• Take control of the family wealth (within 60 days). • Monitor my financial progress at least semi-annually.	• My husband handled the finances, and I have a vague idea of how he did it. • My accountant is my most trusted advisor, but I am not sure of the others.	
LEGACY	• Arrange my affairs for lifetime giving as I choose (within 180 days). • Arrange my affairs for distribution at my death in line with my desires (within 1 year).	• I give generously to my family as I feel they need it from savings. • My husband and I last reviewed our plan together three years ago.	

SUPERPLAN® STRATEGY DECISION WORKSHEET

	SMART GOAL (Restated)	PRESENT SITUATION	STRATEGY
LIFESTYLE	• Maintain my current standard of living indefinitely. • Take two weeks vacation every quarter beginning this quarter.	• I have a general idea of my monthly lifestyle need but am not sure how I can support it. • Travel money can be taken as needed from savings.	• Utilize permanent sources of lifestyle income that do not erode investment principal. • Utilize permanent sources of travel funding that do not erode investment savings/ principal.
PORTFOLIO	• Take control of the family wealth (within 60 days). • Monitor my financial progress at least semi-annually.	• My husband handled the finances, and I have a vague idea of how he did it. • My accountant is my most trusted advisor, but I am not sure of the others.	• Establish and comply with a family investment policy. • Assemble and maintain a collaborative advisory team and meet with them regularly.
LEGACY	• Arrange my affairs for lifetime giving as I choose (within 180 days). • Arrange my affairs for distribution at my death in line with my desires (within 1 year).	• I give generously to my family as I feel they need it from savings. • My husband and I last reviewed our plan together three years ago.	• Utilize permanent sources of discretionary income or assets for gifting that won't jeopardize my lifestyle. • Establish a personal estate plan in line with my desires and update regularly.

As former *National Geographic* photographer Dewitt Jones loves to say, "There are a thousand ways to come at a problem. So many things change when you come at the world with the perspective that there's more than one right answer." His motivational videos and published photographs offer countless examples of how to change perspective, how to reframe a problem into an opportunity. The key is not stopping at your first right answer. Instead go on to find other right answers.

The way you described your present situation will suggest possible solutions. You and your trusted advisor will ask: What if we did it this way? Or what if we did it that way? How would this strategy affect the other goals or strategies? For example, the widow who filled out the sample worksheet had developed tremendous event planning expertise as a volunteer. To help maintain her current standard of living, she could have accepted an attractive job offer at a major organization. However, choosing this strategy would have conflicted with her goal to take two weeks of vacation every quarter.

You and your advisor will list many possible strategies. As you work through this brainstorming exercise, your best alternatives will surface. Write out the best ones in the third column of your worksheet.

The Bonus: Mastering Goal Cultivation

You may be surprised to learn that many of our clients have grown wealthy and even reached financial independence without charting a course for how they'll deal with a major life event transition. In fact, in reviewing our client base, we found that less than half our client families had come to us so they could plan proactively. Most didn't come to us until they had experienced a major life event. Even when someone comes to us because they want to plan proactively, it usually takes them about a year to establish an initial plan and begin to implement it.

So if you've been feeling a bit sheepish during this goal setting phase—maybe even wondering, "Sheesh! Does everyone else but me know how to do this well?"—relax. Let go of any anxiety. Many surviving spouses have waited to really address their goals until they were in your shoes. Some never do.

What you want to do is take some credit for how far you've come, focus on what you are achieving, and feel some confidence for knowing how to work with your trusted advisor and the rest of your advisory team.

You've heard the old saying, "Give a man a fish and you feed him today. Teach a man to fish, and you feed him for life." It's the same with goal setting. So far you've been involved in a linear process. You've been setting and charting goals one at a time.

But did you realize you've also been developing a new skill? The linear process of goal setting has given you the basic experience you need for cultivating a whole garden of goals. You are now prepared to cultivate multiple goals in multiple categories simultaneously. It can actually be dangerous to have only one or two goals. For example, it's possible to let a single goal drive you—even if reaching it costs you your family or your life. Perhaps you know or can imagine someone so tragically single-minded.

But goal cultivators have many goals that balance their lives. Just as a vegetable gardener plants different vegetables—each with different requirements, growth patterns, and harvest dates—so a goal cultivator has many varied goals. The gardener focuses on particular crops in turn, deciding what is best for each, and acting according-ly. This all takes place while tending to neighboring plants, the garden as a whole, and the gardener herself.

Completing this major and final step of the *Planning* phase has positioned you for the *Operating* phase. It may be hard to believe, but you are now ready for action, ready to begin operating your life at a whole new level.

CHAPTER TEN

Operate Step 7 — Time for Action

The world needs dreamers,
the world needs doers, but most of all
the world needs dreamers who do.

— *Sarah Ban Breathnach*

At last! All your plans and preparation are coming to fruition. It's time for action. You are now entering the operating phase, the third of three main phases that make up a healthy transition process. The *Operating* phase has two steps, and in this chapter, you will also identify all the implementers of your plan.

You will decide who will do what, when they will do it, and who will verify that the proper action has been done. Working through the exercise in this chapter will provide you with a "to do" list that will help you begin to truly live your life the way that you want. You have clear goals and a plan to achieve them. You are in control.

The Next Page in Ginny's Story

Remember reading in Chapter Seven about Ginny who decided to move to a smaller house? This choice helped her live within her means. It also pushed her adult children to move out and take responsibility for their lives.

Ginny did all the brainstorming and decision making necessary in the three-step planning phase. By the time she reached the operating phase, she had a clear vision for the legacy she wanted to leave. "I want to minimize estate taxes, and I want to maximize the amount of my estate that goes to those I care about," she told us.

She had learned how to live within her means, and with the help of her trusted advisor and team, mastered her cash flow and managed her investments portfolio—Ginny now knew her estate would be worth millions and that the Internal Revenue Service was set to get more than a third when she passed away.

After comparing alternative strategies, she settled on her best alternative—establishing a series of trusts that would all but eliminate her estate tax and provide for herself, while alive, and for family members and charities of her choice at her passing. In the first step of the operating phase, she determined the best action for carrying out this strategy. She identified who would help her contribute her assets into the various trusts, how much she would put in, when it would happen, how it would happen, and who would verify it.

Completing the Superplan® Action worksheet gave Ginny a tremendous feeling of accomplishment. Though she did not have to perform every detail of her family legacy plan, she chose how to delegate each task and to whom. The action worksheet helped her create the to do-list that gave her a "big picture" of who was accountable for what.

List Vital Actions

Take a minute to study the blank Superplan® Action worksheet on the next page. Finishing your own worksheet can be easy, fun, and satisfying. You have now become familiar with this methodology and can simply transfer the second and third columns from last chapter's worksheet to this chapter's worksheets first and second columns.

Now use the partially completed example on the following page to spur your own thinking. This is the time to tweak any strategy that you might want to restate.

SUPERPLAN® ACTION WORKSHEET

	SMART GOAL (Restated)	STRATEGY (Restated)	ACTION
LIFESTYLE	•	•	•
	•	•	•
PORTFOLIO	•	•	•
	•	•	•
LEGACY	•	•	•
	•	•	•

SUPERPLAN® ACTION WORKSHEET

	SMART GOAL (Restated)	STRATEGY (Restated)	ACTION
LIFESTYLE	• Maintain my current standard of living indefinitely. • Take two weeks vacation every quarter beginning this quarter.	• Utilize permanent sources of lifestyle income that do not erode investment principal. • Utilize permanent sources of travel funding that do not erode investment savings/principal.	
PORTFOLIO	• Take control of the family wealth (within 60 days). • Monitor my financial progress at least semi-annually.	• Establish and comply with a family investment policy. • Assemble and maintain a collaborative advisory team and meet with them regularly.	
LEGACY	• Arrange my affairs for lifetime giving as I choose (within 180 days). • Arrange my affairs for distribution at my death in line with my desires (within 1 year).	• Utilize permanent sources of discretionary income or assets for gifting that won't jeopardize my lifestyle. • Establish a personal estate plan in line with my desires and update regularly.	

The actions you describe may depend on the changes and possibilities you have experienced and glimpsed during your journey across the Widow's Bridge®. For example, in the next completed worksheet, look at the *Legacy* category. The widow established a SMART goal of arranging her affairs for distribution at her death in line with her desires. She wanted this completed within one year. She decided that the best strategy would include making regular updates of her personal estate plan. After all, she already knew how the "life-event big-spin wheel" could create rough waters. That's why she specified this action: "Reconsider existing estate plan in light of recent life events and experiences."

SUPERPLAN® ACTION WORKSHEET

	SMART GOAL *(Restated)*	STRATEGY *(Restated)*	ACTION
LIFESTYLE	• Maintain my current standard of living indefinitely. • Take two weeks vacation every quarter beginning this quarter.	• Utilize permanent sources of lifestyle income that do not erode investment principal. • Utilize permanent sources of travel funding that do not erode investment savings/principal.	• Create a lifestyle cash flow reporting and monitoring process. • Incorporate travel expenditures into cash flow report.
PORTFOLIO	• Take control of the family wealth (within 60 days). • Monitor my financial progress at least semi-annually.	• Establish and comply with a family investment policy. • Assemble and maintain a collaborative advisory team and meet with them regularly.	• Develop and write a family investment policy in line with the "Prudent Investor" guidelines. • Assess current advisory team strengths and weaknesses.
LEGACY	• Arrange my affairs for lifetime giving as I choose (within 180 days). • Arrange my affairs for distribution at my death in line with my desires (within 1 year).	• Utilize permanent sources of discretionary income or assets for gifting that won't jeopardize my lifestyle. • Establish a personal estate plan in line with my desires and update regularly.	• Determine amount of funds available for gifting/donating. • Reconsider existing estate plan in light of recent life events and experiences.

Create Your Action To-Do List

An action won't happen unless you know who will do it, what they are to do, and when they'll do it. Of course, you are already aware that you need to write out your SMART goals. To make sure your actions get implemented, you will want to fill out the Superplan® Action To-Do List, located on the next page.

Feel free to get in the nitty gritty of delegation in the worksheet. Study the first restated action in the example on the page following in the *Portfolio* category. She has chosen to develop and write a family investment policy in line with the "prudent investor" guidelines. On her to-do list, she assigns this action to herself, her CPA (who is also her trusted advisor), and her investment advisor who helped her write the goal. Notice how specifically she describes what this action involves: "Determine objectives, time horizons, assumptions, risk tolerance, asset allocation, and procedures." And she wants to complete this action within 60 days.

It may sound like a lot of work, especially considering that it's just one of many actions on her to-do list. But considering the magnitude of her assets and what's at stake for her future, isn't it a blessing that she has a handle on her situation and someone to help her? You can experience the same clear feeling of control when you and your trusted advisor complete your to-do list.

SUPERPLAN® ACTION TO-DO LIST

ACTION (Restated)	WHO	WHAT	WHEN
LIFESTYLE • •	• •	• •	• •
PORTFOLIO • •	• •	• •	• •
LEGACY • •	• •	• •	• •

SUPERPLAN® ACTION TO-DO LIST

ACTION (Restated)	WHO	WHAT	WHEN
LIFESTYLE • Create lifestyle cash flow reporting process. • Incorporate travel expenditures into cash flow report.			
PORTFOLIO • Develop and write a family investment policy in line with prudent investor guidelines. • Assess current advisory team strengths and weaknesses.			
LEGACY • Determine amount of funds available for gifting/donating. • Reconsider existing estate plan in light of recent life events and experiences.			

Now is the time, with the help of your trusted advisor, to delegate to the team members who will be accountable for what, by when. The following page shows you a good example of how to have your plan ready for action.

SUPERPLAN™ ACTION TO DO LIST

	ACTION (Restated)	WHO	WHAT	WHEN
LIFESTYLE	• Create lifestyle cash flow reporting process. • Incorporate travel expenditures into cash flow report.	• Widow/CPA* • Widow/CPA*	• List actual past 12 months income/expenses and create next year's budget. • Project quarterly travel expenses and add to budget.	• 30 days • 30 days
PORTFOLIO	• Develop and write a family investment policy in line with prudent investor guidelines. • Assess current advisory team strengths and weaknesses.	• Widow/CPA*; Investment Advisor • Widow/CPA*; Investment Advisor, Estate Planning Attorney, Banker, Personal Attorney, etc.	• Determine objectives, time horizon, assumptions, risk tolerance, asset allocation and procedures. • Utilize trusted advisor formula to determine suitability.	• 60 days • 60 days
LEGACY	• Determine amount of funds available for gifting/donating. • Reconsider existing estate plan in light of recent life events and experiences.	• Widow/CPA*; Investment Advisor, etc. • Widow/CPA*; Estate Planning Attorney, etc.	• Establish gifting guidelines/procedures and limitations. • Explore options/outcomes of appropriate alternatives.	• 90 days • 180 days

* Your Most Trusted Advisor

Looking back on the time of your spouse's death, you may find it hard to believe how much progress you've made. Only one step remains to finalize your transition to your new role of family matriarch. Now that you have developed an action list for implementing your plan, it's important to set how you will measure progress as you operate your plan.

CHAPTER ELEVEN

Operate Step 8 — Measure the Progress

The only evidence of growth is change.

— Unknown

Congratulations! You are in the final step of the final phase of your Widow's Bridge® transition. You have written and begun implementing your new life plan. In this chapter, you will learn how to measure the progress and adapt accordingly. This process includes linking accountability and action, evaluating visible results, identifying new capabilities and opportunities—and setting reasonable expectations. Let's start with those expectations.

Dreams and Deadlines

If you believe in the power of possibility, then, in a way, there are no unrealistic goals. But there may be unrealistic deadlines and expectations. Productivity guru Stephen

Covey identifies "sharpen the saw" as one of seven essential habits of highly effective people. He describes this core competency as continuously learning about and improving on your ability to achieve a balanced life.

A woodcutter cannot sharpen a saw and be done with it. After all, there are always more trees to cut, more cabins and chairs to build—more possibilities. So the woodcutter must continually sharpen the saw. In the same way, you can't really set a deadline for "arriving" at your new life. If you are open to life's many right answers, then you will see why dreams sometimes shift—requiring new plans, actions, and deadlines.

This is another way of saying that you have every right to expect progress in implementing your new life plan. However, it is not reasonable to expect that the actual results will always match your ideal. Also, getting results will likely take time. That's why we recommend you do the following exercise after giving your plan a year or so to measure your results.

Take a moment to familiarize yourself with the illustration on the next page. Once again, begin by restating your SMART goals in the first column, refer to the example on the page following.

Note: Free, print-ready Superplan® forms can be obtained from www.widowsbridge.com.

SUPERPLAN® PROGRESS REPORTER (1 YEAR LATER)

	SMART GOAL (Restated)	PROGRESS TO DATE	FINANCIAL IMPACT	NEW CAPABILITIES/ POSSIBILITIES
LIFESTYLE				
PORTFOLIO				
LEGACY				

SUPERPLAN™ PROGRESS REPORTER (1 YEAR LATER)

	SMART GOAL *(Restated)*	PROGRESS TO DATE	FINANCIAL IMPACT	NEW CAPABILITIES/ POSSIBILITIES
LIFESTYLE	• Maintain my current standard of living indefinitely. • Take two weeks vacation every quarter beginning this quarter.			
PORTFOLIO	• Take control of the family wealth (within 60 days). • Monitor my financial progress at least semi-annually.			
LEGACY	• Arrange my affairs for lifetime giving as I choose (within 180 days). • Arrange my affairs for distribution at my death in line with my desires (within 1 year).			

Accountability and Action

Our sample widow's Superplan® Progress Report demonstrates how complicated this life planning stuff can be. No wonder she depends on a trusted advisor and team of other experts. And no wonder she wants to keep a "big picture" overview of who is accountable for what. There's a lot at stake—her present, her future, and her family's legacy.

The second column, Progress To Date, describes how well everyone carried out the actions listed on the Superplan® Action worksheet. For example, the widow's second *Portfolio* goal is to monitor her financial progress at least semi-annually. When she described her situation last year at the beginning of the year, she wrote, "My accountant is my trusted advisor, but I am not sure of the rest of my team members." So she decided her best strategy would be to assemble and maintain a collaborative advisory team and meet with them regularly. And her best action for achieving this *Portfolio* goal would be to "assess current advisory team strengths and weaknesses." Her to-do list specified that her team would include an investment advisor, two lawyers, and a banker; and she would determine their suitability according to the "trusted advisor formula." She gave herself 60 days to complete this assessment.

By looking at the *Portfolio* Progress To Date box on the next page, you can see that the widow determined that not everyone on her initial team was ideal for helping her achieve her portfolio goals, so she restructured the team. That's accountability in action. She knew she didn't have all the knowledge or right relationships necessary to manage her vast portfolio by herself, but she knew what had to be done and kept track of who was accountable for what.

Measuring Visible Results

In the example's *Portfolio* Financial Impact box on the next page following, the widow's Superplan® Progress Reporter clearly shows she has a handle on results. Replacing members of her investment advisory team cost money. In fact, fees for the new team were $30,000 more than for the previous team, but she made excellent choices. The new collaboration saved her $65,000 on income taxes; and when she subtracted her increased fees, she realized a net profit of $35,000 in the first year alone.

SUPERPLAN™ PROGRESS REPORTER (1 YEAR LATER)

	SMART GOAL (Restated)	PROGRESS TO DATE	FINANCIAL IMPACT	NEW CAPABILITIES/ POSSIBILITIES
LIFESTYLE	• Maintain my current standard of living indefinitely. • Take two weeks vacation every quarter beginning this quarter.	• Adapted lifestyle to live within means; current cash flow surplus of $1,000 per month. • Took 4 two-week vacations.		
PORTFOLIO	• Take control of the family wealth (within 60 days). • Monitor my financial progress at least semi-annually.	• Repositioning investment assets in line with family investment policy. • Restructured advisory team adding some members and letting some go.		
LEGACY	• Arrange my affairs for lifetime giving as I choose (within 180 days). • Arrange my affairs for distribution at my death in line with my desires (within 1 year).	• Decided upon maximum annual gifting amount and incorporated it into monthly expense budget. • Retitled both use and investment assets to comply with the terms of the living trust, and updated terms of survivor trust.		

SUPERPLAN™ PROGRESS REPORTER (1 YEAR LATER)

	SMART GOAL *(Restated)*	PROGRESS TO DATE	FINANCIAL IMPACT	NEW CAPABILITIES/ POSSIBILITIES
LIFESTYLE	• Maintain my current standard of living indefinitely. • Take two weeks vacation every quarter beginning this quarter.	• Adapted lifestyle to live within means; current cash flow surplus of $1,000 per month. • Took 4 two-week vacations.	• $1,000/mo to savings = $12,000 this year. • $24,000 from cash flow did not reduce portfolio.	
PORTFOLIO	• Take control of the family wealth (within 60 days). • Monitor my financial progress at least semi-annually.	• Repositioning investment assets in line with family investment policy. • Restructured advisory team adding some members and letting some go.	• Portfolio total return of 7% vs. 5% during previous period equals $20,000 per $1M per year. • Fees for new team were $30,000 more than previous team; collaboration generated $65,000 income tax saving resulting in a net profit of $35,000.	
LEGACY	• Arrange my affairs for lifetime giving as I choose (within 180 days). • Arrange my affairs for distribution at my death in line with my desires (within 1 year).	• Decided upon maximum annual gifting amount and incorporated it into monthly expense budget. • Retitled both use and investment assets to comply with the terms of the living trust, and updated terms of survivor trust.	• $20,000 from cash flow did not reduce portfolio. • Bypass trust isolates $1.5M from estate tax at second death, resulting in a tax savings of $750,000.	

This clearly stated visible result also shows what planning with a trusted advisor and a process can help you achieve. Remember that this widow's trusted advisor provided the formula to help her assess her investment advisory team, and the change paid off big time. You will also want to enlist your trusted advisor when you fill out your Superplan® Progress Reporter.

As you work through the first three columns, look back on where you were when you started and where you actually are when you're measuring. Knowing where you want to be is important, but understand your horizon changes regularly as you continually move forward. Gauge your progress by looking at the actual improvement along the way. Take a mental snapshot of where you were. Then, one year or so later, take another mental snapshot of where you are. When you compare the two, it's much easier to see how far you've come than thinking about what's left to do.

So if you still feel dissatisfied while filling out this chapter's worksheet, try going back to Chapter Nine. Read through how you described your present situation then and think again about where you are now. You just might say, "Oh! I accomplished a lot more than I realized!" When our clients calculate the financial impact of planning and implementing for one year and figure in the fees paid to their advisory team, their return on investment usually averages many times the fees.

Identifying New Capabilities and Possibilities

Filling out the fourth column on your Superplan® Progress Reporter allows you to build on your progress. With your newfound confidence that you are in control of your life and have enough money to maintain your lifestyle, you can embellish on any success you've achieved and start thinking of new capabilities and possibilities.

SUPERPLAN™ PROGRESS REPORTER (1 YEAR LATER)

	SMART GOAL *(Restated)*	PROGRESS TO DATE	FINANCIAL IMPACT	NEW CAPABILITIES/ POSSIBILITIES
LIFESTYLE	• Maintain my current standard of living indefinitely. • Take two weeks vacation every quarter beginning this quarter.	• Adapted lifestyle to live within means; current cash flow surplus of $1,000 per month. • Took 4 two-week vacations.	• $1,000/mo to savings = $12,000 this year. • $24,000 from cash flow did not reduce portfolio.	• Experience of controlling income and expenditures can be utilized as a basis for all future financial decision making. • Current and future earnings available for reinvesting or inclusion in lifestyle expenditures.
PORTFOLIO	• Take control of the family wealth (within 60 days). • Monitor my financial progress at least semi-annually.	• Repositioning investment assets in line with family investment policy. • Restructured advisory team adding some members and letting some go.	• Portfolio total return of 7% vs. 5% during previous period equals $20,000 per $1M per year. • Fees for new team were $30,000 more than previous team; collaboration generated $65,000 income tax saving resulting in a net profit of $35,000.	• Confidence in diversified portfolio and the ability to generate more income if desired. • Confidence in team's ability to meet challenge of change and capitalize on money saving opportunities.
LEGACY	• Arrange my affairs for lifetime giving as I choose (within 180 days). • Arrange my affairs for distribution at my death in line with my desires (within 1 year).	• Decided upon maximum annual gifting amount and incorporated it into monthly expense budget. • Retitled both use and investment assets to comply with the terms of the living trust, and updated terms of survivor trust.	• $20,000 from cash flow did not reduce portfolio. • Bypass trust isolates $1.5M from estate tax at second death, resulting in a tax savings of $750,000.	• Gifts can be made at the donor's discretion up to the maximum allotted amount, and can be adjusted as funds become restricted or available. • Even though assets are no longer titled to the survivor, all income from the trust is available to the survivor.

For example, in the completed report on the previous page, follow each column's entry for the second *Lifestyle* item. You'll notice that this widow spent $24,000 on four two-week vacations—without reducing her portfolio principal. She now realizes that, if she wants to, she can easily afford to keep traveling at the same style. But she might also tell herself, "You know what? Those vacations were fun, but now I'd like to do something different with my current and future earnings. I want to remodel the kitchen. Or maybe I'd rather invest in my nephew's company."

For you, too, a brighter future will become ever more clear as you write out your new capabilities and possibilities. Perhaps you'll decide to seek employment and add the income to your lifestyle cash flow. Maybe you'll get excited about your growing ability to take care of your community, whether through volunteering, charitable giving, or a revised legacy plan.

The point is that the steps you completed in the previous chapters are ones you can do again and again. Each time you compare where you were to where you now are, you'll see how far you've come. Then you can go right back and fill out another Superplan® Future Focus worksheet (Chapter Eight) and work on creating a new updated vision.

This exercise can be the foundation of an open-ended habit of an upward spiral of progress. You can decide how steep you want the spiral to be or how fast to go around. We recommend doing it on a regular cycle. Pulling your planning team together for this process each year is a helpful discipline in and of itself.

In going through the Widow's Bridge® process, I hope it has reaffirmed your ability to create and re-create your life. You may have also noticed a strategic pattern of positioning. This positioning has been done to lead you to the ultimate life step—living with significance.

CHAPTER TWELVE

Live with Significance

Growth itself contains the germ of happiness.

— Pearl Buck

You have now experienced the Widow's Bridge® process. Hopefully, you've begun to realize a new dimension of your own power to create and re-create your life. You are poised to move from personal success (what's good for you and your family) to personal significance (what's good for your community and the world at large).

Before we get into how you can define your personal style of significance, there's a vital question I'd like you to ask yourself. Given that you've read this far in the book, the question may strike you as almost strange, but please think it over and answer honestly.

Have You Chosen to Move On?

In both our research and our decades of working with widows, we've noticed that, eventually, every widow makes a choice. Some continue to live a lifestyle shaped by the traps and loops of widowhood. Let's call them Group A. Others choose to work with what's available and move toward a brighter future. Let's call them Group B.

The widows in Group A maintain an indefinite state of restrictive grief at some level. They stay stuck in feelings of sadness, woe, and persecution. Group A widows often tell us the following things, or they live as if these beliefs are true.

- "It's not fair."—It's normal to feel shocked and angry when your husband dies. After all, that's not what you wanted or expected from life. Some widows never get past these feelings. They remain angry for years.

- "He's still here."—Denial is a natural stage of grief. Only those who have lived though it know what it's like to experience a loss so painful that they can't bear to face it. They pretend for a little while that the pain didn't happen. Some widows carry this step too far. For example, a CPA that I know is acquainted with a woman who still has her husband's clothes hanging in their bedroom closet. The man died 15 years ago, and she continues to pretend he is still here.

- "He's coming back."—When someone has been such an important part of your life, you may feel disloyal to think of or plan for life without that person. Many

Group A widows deal with this by going through the motions of planning for the future; yet, they live as if their husbands are not dead, just gone for a while. By behaving as if their husbands are really coming back, these unfortunate women simply tread water.

By contrast, the widows in Group B eventually manage to accept things the way they are. They work through the shock, denial, fear, anger, grief, and everything else associated with losing a spouse to death. At some point they assess where they are—and then decide to go somewhere brighter.

They choose to follow a process like the one you've read about in previous chapters. They work through their grief at their own pace and in their own way. Some choose a trusted advisor and a team to help them become self-sufficient in managing lifestyle cash flow, taking control of their investment portfolios, settling their husbands' estates, and developing a family legacy plan. Through each step, they follow a *stabilize-plan-operate* strategy. Some go it alone.

You probably know in your heart whether you've chosen to move on. If you're not sure, though, here's a simple way to reveal your inner choice: How do you usually answer someone who asks you when your husband died? Do you say something like "I've been a widow for 15 years (Group A)"? Or is your reply more like "I was widowed 15 years ago (Group B)"?

The difference between those replies is subtle but powerful. Group A women define themselves as widows, now and forever. Group B women describe their husband's death, the event that widowed them, as a traumatic, life-changing experience. That event profoundly shaped them. However, they have also chosen to take control and be responsible for their future. Have you?

Define Your Personal Style of Significance

The late Joan Kroc was a shining example of how to live with significance. Her husband, McDonald's restaurant founder Ray Kroc, died in 1984. She then made a deliberate choice. He left her with so much money that taking care of her family was easy. She decided to devote the rest of her life to philanthropy.

You've probably read about the many causes she gave to, including world peace, education, homeless shelters, public radio, and the Salvation Army. More often than not, she gave anonymously. Many organizations and people didn't learn that she was their benefactor until after the heiress died on October 12, 2003. Joan Kroc found significance in supporting causes she believed in, not in having other people know that she had made big gifts.

On the other hand, plenty of generous people find that publicly lending their name to a cause helps generate more gifts from their peers. The point here is not to prescribe a way of giving but to describe some of the many ways that widows have developed their personal styles of significance.

Even though you probably don't have billions, once you, like Joan Kroc, have decided to move on after your husband's death and have reached personal success, you'll want to go to the next level regarding your legacy. Some widows get a great deal of satisfaction from amassing and preserving a fortune to bequeath to their families or charity. That may not be the way you feel. What will your legacy be?

Martha's Story

One of our clients, a widow I'll call Martha, worked with us after her husband's death. By the second anniversary of her husband's death, she was comfortably stable. She remarried about three years after being widowed.

A little before her remarriage, after we'd gone over her financial affairs, I said, "Well, that about sizes it up. Is there anything else you've been thinking of?"

She replied, "What do you mean?"

"Well," I asked. "Are you fulfilled?"

She smiled and shook her head. "Funny you should ask," she said. "I've been thinking about that. I'm not."

"So, what's missing?" I asked.

Martha thought a bit. "I want to help someone else. I've had a wonderful life. Now I want to give back. I want to help others who need it. But who are they?"

We decided that her assignment before our next meeting was to go out and look around. She would look for causes or organizations that lit her fire. She came back excited about a nonprofit organization that advocates for neglected and abused children. Martha didn't devote her entire life to this cause, but she did put time and energy into it, and she got a lot of satisfaction out of those gifts. She also made an arrangement, small but significant, to benefit the organization through her estate plan.

Many people dream of making a difference. No matter what your financial state, you actually have the means to do it. Give yourself a time period—take as much time as you need, but do set a deadline—during which you pay special attention to the needs in the community or world around you. You might keep a journal or jot down your thoughts about the following issues.

What news stories capture your attention? Which people or causes raise your pulse or put you near tears? Listen carefully when you hear about needs from your family, friends, neighbors, or faith community. Do you want to right a wrong, give to a specific cause, provide an unexpected gift to a family facing grim odds? Can you recall a time when you wanted to give to something or someone and didn't feel you had the freedom to do so? Do you have that freedom now?

By the end of your self-imposed deadline as you find your passion, you'll have excellent ideas about how you can use your blessings to create your own personal style of significance. It's a skill you can continue to develop for the rest of your life. No advisor can possibly calculate your return on that investment. Only you will know.

The Greatest Club No One Wants to Join

I recently interviewed another widow, one only 43 years old. She told me she was on her way to dinner with a group of widows who all live in one of the most upscale communities in greater San Diego.

In describing the event, she said, "Everyone in our dinner group is a widow under 50. We don't talk a lot about being widows. We just all have this experience in common. Instead we just get together to share a meal and a great time.

"One woman in our group started referring to our get-togethers as 'the greatest club no one wants to join,'" she told me.

The greatest club no one wants to join. Think about that. Just as the fire-ravaged forest grows back with a maturity it could only get from surviving the event, these women have a new perspective and new growth that would not have been possible without living through their common experience.

Although you did not choose to be widowed, you have many choices about how to live your life from this day forward. We hope that this book gives you a taste of the solidarity you may find as you cross your Widow's Bridge to a brighter future.

Conclusion

The plan is nothing; the planning is everything.

— Winston Churchill

Welcome to the other side. You have bridged the Widow's Plight Gap. Numerous times, many different widows have said, "You cannot possibly know what it feels like (to be a widow) unless you have actually experienced it." I hope the journey through this book has given you some insight into the situation. If you are not a widow, then neither you nor I can truly understand at this time. However, we can talk about what to do to prepare and be proactive about your future.

Oddly enough, the preparation for what has been labeled the single most stressful life event by far—the loss of a spouse—can actually improve your existing marital relationship and create a better life for you today. It has been said that planning brings order and success into one's life. You have probably already noticed that your spouse doesn't have to die in order to complete the last five steps (the Superplan®) of the Widow's Bridge® process.

Having a comprehensive personal financial plan in place, such as the Superplan® outlined in the book, can go a long way toward preparing you to bridge the gap. Also, though the technology certainly exists and some people today are perfectly content doing their own financial planning, the benefits of working with a third party, professional financial advisor are significant. To name a few, someone who is familiar with the estate planning process can not only help you design a plan that is right for you and your family, but they can help keep you on track to complete it and keep it up to date—as Ruth on the very first page of this book so clearly demonstrates. The greatest plan in the world is worthless without implementing the formal documentation that memorializes your intentions.

Identifying a team of qualified advisors and a trusted advisor that both you and your spouse are comfortable with may be the most difficult challenge of all. How can you possibly trust someone without working with them through your issues and observing the manner in which they respond to you? How can they possibly get to know you well enough to be effective on your behalf without spending the time with you to empathize with your feelings? Mutual trust relationships are built over time with everyone involved interacting while dealing with real life issues. This is the heart of the matter—to find someone you are very comfortable with, so that when the unthinkable happens, you have your trusted advisor in place to hold your hand and walk with you across the Widow's Bridge®.

Start today organizing your team—your "three-legged stool". Identify the people you are working with now that you can truly trust. Ask yourself, "Who is missing?" You may even want to go through the exercise, "Let's pretend it happened last week." Who would you depend on today? Who would you turn to and ask, "What do I do now?" Who would hold your hand for the first two years as you cross over your Widow's Bridge®?

As the popular commercial goes, "Just do it." Think of this acronym, **DO IT**, to motivate you to get started.

1. **D**evelop a relationship with a trusted advisor now.
2. **O**rganize your Cash Flow, Portfolio, and Legacy (Focus).
3. **I**dentify your priorities (Decide).
4. **T**ake Action by implementing your plan (Act).

The obvious benefits are many, as are the not-so-obvious ones. I've been told the personal interaction of the "let's pretend" exercise has actually strengthened marriages.

The barriers to acting now are also formidable. Even in the information age, no one wants to talk about death. That is denial in its purest sense. Also, we are all very busy. Estate planning is one of those things that is important, not urgent, and therefore easy to put off over and over again, especially when we are relatively young.

Whatever your barrier, for some reason you were inspired to pick up this book. Draw upon that motivation to take the next logical step that's right for you. Talk to an existing advisor or a friend you feel might "have it all together". Ask them what they would do to get started if they were you. Don't stop until you feel you are making real progress. Only you know what will satisfy your concerns. Just do whatever it takes to make it happen. The resulting confidence and peace of mind, not to mention the family stability and money at stake, will make it all worthwhile.

Share your wisdom. Whether you use this plan to prepare for the unthinkable, or you have already experienced that loss, please let me know how you find the Widow's Bridge® process helpful. I would especially like to hear your stories. Your story may provide someone else a source of comfort, courage, and confidence. You may also have other suggestions for how trusted advisors can be more helpful.

Please accept my invitation to visit our website at www.widowsbridge.com. You will find a fantastic list of books that will help you with health, emotional, and financial issues. You can also print fresh copies of the Superplan® worksheets.

You have my heartfelt wishes for all the best life has to offer. As with anything else in life, a little preparation goes a long way toward reaching your goals. Thank you for allowing me to help you in this very important, personal matter.

For additional information you can also visit www.superplan.com.

ROBERT D. REED PUBLISHERS ORDER FORM
Call in your order for fast service and quantity discounts
(541) 347-9882

OR order on-line at **www.rdrpublishers.com** *using PayPal.*

OR order by mail: **Make copies of this form;** *enclose payment information:*

Robert D. Reed Publishers
1380 Face Rock Drive, Bandon, OR 97411

Note: Shipping is $3.50 1st book + $1 for each additional book.

Send indicated books to:

Name _____

Address _____

City _____ State _____ Zip _____

Phone: _____ Fax: _____ Cell: _____

E-Mail: _____

Check #_____ or credit card: Visa _____ MasterCard_____Other_____

Name on card _____

Card Number _____

Exp. Date _____ Last 3-Digit number on back of card: _____

Qty.

The Coming Widow Boom: *What You and Your Loved Ones Can Do to Prepare for the Unthinkable* by James F. "Buddy" Thomas, Jr. ....$14.95 _____

Preparing Heirs: *Five Steps to a Successful Transition of Family Wealth and Values* By Roy Williams & Vic Preisser ....$29.95 _____

Philanthropy, Heirs & Values By Roy Williams & Vic Preisser ....$29.95 _____

RelationShift: Revolutionary Fundraising by Michael Bassoff &Steve Chandler .... $11.95 _____

The Small Business Millionire by Steve Chandler & Sam Beckford.. $11.95 _____

Customer Astonishment: 10 Secrets to World-Class Customer Care by Darby Checketts .... $14.95 _____

Other book title(s) from website, www.rdrpublishers.com:

_____ $_____ _____

_____ $_____ _____

TOTAL AMOUNT OF ORDER: $_____